Taurus
21 April – 21 May

DID YOU PURCHASE THIS BOOK WITHOUT A COVER?
If you did, you should be aware it is **stolen property** as it was
reported *unsold and destroyed* by a retailer. Neither the author nor
the publisher has received any payment for this book.

*All Rights Reserved including the right of reproduction in whole or
in part in any form. This edition is published by arrangement with
Harlequin Enterprises II B.V./S.à.r.l. The text of this publication or
any part thereof may not be reproduced or transmitted in any form
or by any means, electronic or mechanical, including photocopying,
recording, storage in an information retrieval system, or otherwise,
without the written permission of the publisher.*

*This book is sold subject to the condition that it shall not, by way of
trade or otherwise, be lent, resold, hired out or otherwise circulated
without the prior consent of the publisher in any form of binding or
cover other than that in which it is published, and without a similar
condition including this condition being imposed on the subsequent
purchaser.*

® *and* ™ *are trademarks owned and used by the trademark owner
and/or its licensee. Trademarks marked with* ® *are registered with the
United Kingdom Patent Office and/or the Office for Harmonisation
in the Internal Market and in other countries.*

*First published in Great Britain 2008
by Harlequin Mills & Boon Limited,
Eton House, 18-24 Paradise Road, Richmond, Surrey TW9 1SR*

Copyright © Dadhichi Toth 2007, 2008 & 2009

ISBN: 978 0 263 86905 7

Typeset at Midland Typesetters Australia

*Harlequin Mills & Boon policy is to use papers that are
natural, renewable and recyclable products and made from
wood grown in sustainable forests. The logging and
manufacturing processes conform to the legal environmental
regulations of the country of origin.*

*Printed and bound in Spain
by Litografia Rosés S.A., Barcelona*

About Dadhichi

Dadhichi is one of Australia's foremost astrologers, and is frequently seen on TV and in the media. He has the unique ability to draw from complex astrological theory to provide clear, easily understandable advice and insights for people who want to know what their future may hold.

In the 25 years that Dadhichi has been practising astrology, and conducting face and other esoteric readings, he has provided over 9,000 consultations. His clients include celebrities, political and diplomatic figures and media and corporate identities from all over the world.

Dadhichi's unique blend of astrology and face reading helps people fulfil their true potential. His extensive experience practising western astrology is complemented by his research into the theory and practice of eastern forms of astrology.

Dadhichi has been a guest on many Australian television shows and several of his political and worldwide forecasts have proved uncannily accurate. He has appeared on many of Australia's leading television networks and is a regular columnist for several Australian magazines.

His websites www.astrology.com.au, www.facereader.com and soulmate.com.au which attract hundreds of thousands of visitors each month, offer a wide variety of features, helpful information and services.

Dedicated to The Light of Intuition

Sri V. Krishnaswamy — mentor and friend

With thanks to Julie, Joram, Isaac and Janelle

Welcome from
Dadhichi

Dear Friend,

It's a pleasure knowing you're reading this, your astrological forecast for 2009. There's nothing more exciting than looking forward to a bright new year and considering what the stars have in store and how you might make the most of what's on offer in your life.

Apart from the anticipation of what I might predict will happen to you, of what I say about your upcoming luck and good fortune, remember that astrology is first and foremost a tool of personal growth, self-awareness and inner transformation. What 'happens to us' is truly a reflection of what we're giving out; the signals we are transmitting to our world, our universe.

The astrological adage of 'As above, so below' can also be interpreted in a slightly different way when I say 'As within, so without'! In other words, as hard as it is to believe, the world and our experiences of it, or our relationships and circumstances, good or bad, do tend to mirror our own belief systems and mental patterns.

It is for this reason that I thought I'd write a brief introductory note to remind you that the stars are pointers to your wonderful destiny and that you must work with them to realise your highest and most noble goals. The greatest marvel and secret is your own inner self! Astrology reveals these inner secrets of your character, which are the foundation of your life's true purpose.

What is about to happen to you this year is exciting, but what you *do* with this special power of knowledge, how you share your talents with others, and the way you truly enjoy each moment of your life is far more important than knowing *what* will happen. This is the key to a 'superior' kind of happiness. It will start to open up to you when you live in harmony with your true nature as shown by astrology.

I really hope you enjoy your coming twelve months, and gain new insights and fresh perspectives on your life through studying your 2009 horoscope. Here's hoping great success will be yours and health, love and happiness will follow wherever you go.

I leave you now with the words of a wise man, who once said:

> Sow a thought, and you reap an act;
> Sow an act, and you reap a habit;
> Sow a habit, and you reap a character;
> Sow a character, and you reap a destiny.
> Your thoughts are the architects of your destiny.

Warm regards, and may the stars shine brightly for you in 2009!

Your Astrologer,

Dadhichi Toth

Contents

The Taurus Identity 9

   Taurus: A Snapshot 10

Star Sign Compatibility 27

2009: The Year Ahead 51

2009: Month By Month Predictions 61

   January 62

   February 66

   March 70

   April 74

   May 78

   June 82

July 86

August 90

September 94

October 98

November 102

December 106

2009: Astronumerology 111

2009: Your Daily Planner 133

The Taurus Identity

TAURUS

We are all inventors, each sailing out on a voyage of discovery, guided each by a private chart, of which there is no duplicate. The world is all gates, all opportunities.

—Ralph Waldo Emerson

Taurus: A Snapshot

Key Characteristics

Security conscious, determined, sensual, loyal, steady, proud, obstinate and decisive

Compatible Star Signs

Virgo, Capricorn and Pisces

Key Life Phrase

I have

Life Goals

To be the best and to be first; to be a leader rather than a follower

Platinum Assets

Enthusiasm, inspiration and fearlessness

Zodiac Totem

The Bull

Zodiac Symbol

♉

Zodiac Facts

Second sign of the zodiac; fixed, fruitful, feminine and moist

THE TAURUS IDENTITY

Element

Earth

Famous Taureans

Carmen Electra, Queen Elizabeth II, Yehudi Menuhin, Jack Nicholson, Barbra Streisand, Carol Burnett, Uma Thurman, Joe Lewis, Cher, Andie MacDowell, Al Pacino, Penelope Cruz, Shirley MacLaine, Cate Blanchett, Renee Zellweger, Saddam Hussein, Kirsten Dunst, James Brown, George Clooney and Janet Jackson

Key to karma, spirituality and emotional balance

In your past life Capricorn and its ruler Saturn had a strong influence on you, which led to your desire for security. Your key words are 'I have' and therefore it is important not to let a desire for money and material objects overshadow your true purpose.

You like calm and peaceful environments in which you can get back in touch with your spiritual self. Nature is an excellent environment in which to do this.

Mercury rules Wednesdays and is friendly to your ruler, Venus. Learn to relax more and carry out your meditations on this day. This will accelerate your psychic insights. Take calming baths and use sandalwood, cedarwood and rose oils to help connect with your higher self.

Taurus: Your profile

Don't you get a little tired of people referring to Taurus as stubborn, pig-headed or bullish? I think the more polite way of describing you is determined, persevering and yes, opinionated, but certainly no pushover in an argument once your mind is made up. Am I right or right?

In the extreme, I would say that you do have a tendency to prefer sticking with the tried and true rather than impulsively

TAURUS

moving in a new direction. You have to have a darned good reason to do something; otherwise, yes, you can be a little stubborn.

But this perfectly reflects the practicality of your star sign, the earthy nature of your personality. Such descriptions as prudent and tight-fisted don't worry you because you are primarily concerned about positive results that ensure your future security.

If it comes to making an important life decision you are very much aware of how this impacts upon your loved ones, particularly if you are a family person with children or others who are dependant upon you. You don't want your decisions to be flaky and cause trouble for anyone so you see caution and thoroughness as absolutely essential.

You are an excellent worker and this is because you prefer to do things carefully and properly. You hate cutting corners and doing more than one thing at a time. If you are forced to rush something it really increases your stress levels because you know that doing a job well requires complete focus and attention, and this you have.

However, these positive traits, which centre on your cautious attitude, can sometimes be based on a fear of change and this might not always work to your benefit. Can I recommend you at least listen to what others have to say, even if you don't necessarily agree?

You like to feel as if you're the master of your own destiny and therefore anyone who thinks they are going to push you in this or that direction is very much mistaken. When the bull digs in its heels, no one on Earth can move it. I can see you chuckling as I reveal the obvious to you.

The fact that change is the only constant thing in life is something you don't like being reminded of, but it's not a bad idea for you to prepare yourself for some of the inevitable and

THE TAURUS IDENTITY

unexpected changes so that you're better equipped to deal with them with a minimum of fuss and tension.

You're sometimes far too easygoing for your own good. Some Taureans prefer to leave everything to the last minute and then wonder why they end up reacting so strongly to the unpleasant changes that are going on around them. Be a step ahead of what's happening because you are capable of foresight and good intuition. Don't let complacency throw you off your course.

Taurus is ruled by Venus and this indicates a wonderful taste for aesthetic things, luxurious lifestyle items, fine food and generally the better things in life. You enjoy all of the good things that money can buy, no doubt, but must be extremely careful not to let the excessive side of Venus dominate you. This can have adverse ramifications on your health, wellbeing and also your relationships if you don't take control of it.

You're a very sensitive and patient individual and, even if success doesn't fall into your lap at the outset, it doesn't bother you. You understand the value of appreciating what comes through hard work. You seize the opportunities that arise but only if you can see some practical value in them.

You're a very straightforward individual; in fact, some might call you black and white. Your open mind and honest speech never leaves doubt as to where you stand on any topic.

You don't mind getting your hands dirty, which is why many Taureans like to work in the garden or work with their hands at odd jobs around the home. You're not afraid of hard work and this has to do with the earthy quality of the sign Taurus. Even women aren't scared of those manual jobs that would scare off other zodiac signs in a flash. If you're married to a Taurean woman, you mustn't expect her to do your hard work for you, though. She's a woman who believes in equality of the sexes.

TAURUS

You have a simple yet graceful charm that people are attracted to. Venus has a natural beauty that doesn't need too much embellishment. You also have a strong intuitive feeling about things and prefer to rely on this rather than intellectualising. Your judgement of others is usually quite correct.

Three classes of Taurus

If as a Taurus you are born between 21 and 29 April, you were born with an extra dose of loving Venus energy. This means your love life and romance is extremely important to you; but you must learn that bigger and more expensive does not always mean the best. Attracting someone of means shouldn't be the criterion for whether or not you want to spend the rest of your life with them.

If you were born between 11 and 21 May, you are interested in money and the leverage that it gives you. Being practical and saving for your long-term objectives is a key feature of your personality, but don't forget to smell the roses along the way.

Were you born between 30 April and 10 May? Then I see Mercury stimulating your active mind and also making you a stern critic of both yourself and others. Try to balance your reasoning with your intuition and this will bring you considerably more contentment in life.

Taurus role model: Cate Blanchett

Taurean elegance and practicality is seen reflected perfectly in Australia's famous actress Cate Blanchett. Apart from her stunning screen and stage success, she has joined the fight against global warming and is trying to raise public awareness of the Earth's environmental issues. This again reflects her connectedness to the Earth and her earth sign of Taurus.

THE TAURUS IDENTITY

Taurus: The light side

Venus is your ruler and one of the more desirable planets of the zodiac, endowing you with a down-to-earth sense of humour and wonderful social skills. You're never too highbrow that you won't talk to someone lower down on the social ladder and, in fact, feel quite uncomfortable being made to feel superior. You treat everyone equally and this is a great strength and asset.

Artistic Venus also brings with it a love of art, crafts and a sense of colour, form and beauty to the Taurean temperament. Anything beautiful attracts you and likewise the beauty in you attracts others.

You have a no-frills approach when it comes to helping others and your words are direct and cut straight to the heart of the problem. People always look to you when they need help. In this you are gentle, practical, and always useful.

Your work ethic is exemplary and you believe that even a menial task should be carried out with care and precision. You are a perfectionist.

Try to share your talents with those around you, even though you feel as though modesty is desirable. The world will be better for it.

Taurus: The shadow side

One of the most important things for you to understand is that you should delegate and save yourself time and trouble in your daily life. Your inability to allow others to help stems from a lack of trust in your own ability to do things as well.

There may be some truth to this but sooner or later you'll come to realise that no two people do things the same and gradually you'll let go of this habit. This attitude requires flexibility on your part and, although it won't be easy, reducing your rigidity is essential for your growth.

TAURUS

You rule the roost at home and like to show others how it's done. As long as everything is working to your plan you're quite happy, but should someone decide to step outside the square it can throw you out of kilter.

This will annoy others and it becomes a source of tension in your personal life. Let others continue to develop their own abilities and show your appreciation for them without trying to exert your will and dominate the situation.

On the one hand your determination is an excellent Taurean trait but when taken to extremes it will push others away. With honesty you will be able to change your habits.

Taurus woman

It's the sheer determination of the Taurus woman that guarantees success for her. Nothing gets in the way of your dreams once you've set your eye on a specific goal. Your practicality and no-nonsense approach to achieving your objectives is your secret weapon for a successful life.

Hard working and often impervious to other's opinions, there's not much you can't achieve even if others say it can't be done. You can have a singular mind, which, when concentrated, can achieve amazing results.

You understand that sometimes you can't have what you want when you want it. This is where your perseverance pays off. Undaunted by time and the fact that you sometimes have to wait longer than others for your dreams to materialise, your patience wins out in the end.

Femininity is your second name with beautiful Venus bringing out the truly womanly qualities in your personality. You reflect all the softness and gentility that is infused into Taurus by Venus. People are attracted to the way you dress and present yourself and can feel your sensual and loving nature just by being in your company.

THE TAURUS IDENTITY

You have a simple yet elegant way of presenting your character and your style. Always clean, tasteful and in keeping with your age, your fashion statements befit your character. This is pleasing to the eye and also attractive in its own way.

When you don't necessarily have to make an impression you are more than happy to kick back in your casuals and hang loose. This is a time when you can be really 'earthy' and feel more in your element than you care to admit. It basically means you can get among your work and outdoor activities without fear of worrying about getting dirty or messed up. This is a form of relaxation to you.

For you, family life is a must. It's a significant part of fulfilling yourself, so having children will be an important part of your life programme. You are so protective of your loved ones that your children will be your number one priority. Being instinctively nurturing therefore stimulates your love of cooking, entertaining and keeping a clean house, which will become your pride and joy. If you have a stable home life, you'll feel blissfully contented.

You love to care for visitors and friends and will make your home the hub of social activity. A bottle of fine wine and a few exotic new dishes is something you like to prepare for guests, being the excellent hostess that you are.

Whether you're a professional or homemaker you need to have a plan and to work to a tight schedule. Spontaneous actions are not in keeping with your personality so you need to be given ample notice to fit your friends into your routine.

Adept at focusing your attention on one challenge at a time, you're able to achieve much more because you're not easily distracted.

Your opinions are quite fixed and sometimes, even if others offer you a reasonable cause to change your mind, you'll still adhere to your opinions. The challenge for you will

TAURUS

be to relax your views a little and sample a taste of how the other half does things.

Taurus man

Being earthy and grounded individuals, Taurus men are extremely practical in every aspect of their lives. Although the ruling planet for Taurus is Venus, a feminine and sensitive sign, most Taurus men are male through and through.

As a Taurus male, you are slow, plodding and efficient in the use of your energy and this ensures you success and material security over the long-term. You prefer this to anything else and won't tolerate anything that undermines your emotional and mental security, either. Security is a synonym for Taurus.

You're faithful in your relationships and this has to be one of your most attractive traits to the fairer sex. Some women may think you're a little slow off the mark but this is just your way of scouting the territory before putting your heart on the line. You like to see clearly what your potential partner's character is really like before tying the knot.

Taurus men are sometimes traditional, perhaps even old-fashioned in their views, but can never be accused of being unfeeling or superficial in love. You'll be a stable and supportive partner in marriage. You're a great supporter of friends and family alike but on the work front will also be there to offer whatever help you can when it is needed. You're able to shoulder responsibility far better than most others and your commitment to any task is admirable.

Despite the fact that you are a high achiever in life, you take your time throughout the process without cutting corners, even if it takes longer than you'd like it to. Doing the job properly the first time is superior to having to do it over and over again.

THE TAURUS IDENTITY

There is a creative element to your character and if you do have a touch of entertainment flowing through your blood you might find yourself drawn to music, dance and other artistic pursuits. Many great performers were born under the sign of Taurus, including Andie MacDowell, Al Pacino, Penelope Cruz and Renee Zellweger. Coupled with these artistic desires your Taurean commitment to achieving your goals is obviously the perfect blend of energies for success, as in the case of these famous personalities.

You love your children. If you choose a married life you'll nourish them as well as giving them a soft place to land. You will provide material and emotional support for them whenever it is needed. You are inflexible in the extreme and will need to understand the principles of give and take a little more. This will make life so much easier for you and improve your health at the same time!

Try not to make decisions that exclude others from participating, too. Remain open and, if you disagree, be courteous to communicate your reasons for choosing to stick to your guns. This will result in much more respect.

You can become a little worried over money and the issues of security because you hate feeling as if you may have to struggle and may not be able to provide for your loved ones. Try to relax a little more as Taurus rarely has problems making ends meet, even if they're not the wealthiest of people. Your resourcefulness is excellent.

Taurus child

Your Taurus child is absolutely lovable and you can thank the planet Venus for this. Born with a natural charm and humorous streak as well, they'll become your best friend.

Your Taurus child is cuddly and loving, just like Venus. They don't necessarily jump around like jack rabbits all that

TAURUS

much, but they are observant and when dissatisfied will certainly let you know it. If they decide on a course of action, you'd better be prepared to either go with it or give up everything else to fight their determined little minds.

Taurus children need huge amounts of emotional nurturing. You need to pay attention to their shifting moods, which are not always evident on the surface. They may not say anything for days and then explode out of the blue.

Taurus is a touchy-feely sign and therefore Taurean children crave physical affection. Taurus requires this key ingredient in greater measure than others. I do hope that you enjoy the physical contact as much as your Taurean child will enjoy receiving it. If this is the case both of you will be drawn that much closer together.

Taurean children are able to get what they want so you shouldn't be surprised when they butter you up and then tactfully corner you as they go in for the kill. They are pretty hard to resist and in some ways are the perfect sales people in their manner of getting you to give them what they want.

Make sure you give your Taurus child many opportunities to explore the world, to get out into the fresh air and become one with nature. This is essential for their all-round development. Preferably you'll have a garden in your backyard and this will absorb them. If not, make sure you get them to the local park or down to the beach every so often so they can receive the grounding they need through their outdoor physical movement.

Although Taurean children have an active and artistic imagination, they are equally inclined to maths, science and geography. Music is one of their preferred activities, which touches their souls and helps them open their hearts and minds so as to not brood over their feelings. Make certain you encourage these artistic activities and hobbies for them.

THE TAURUS IDENTITY

Taurus children have a large group of friends and they will be the centre of attention in their group. Teach them to value sharing with their friends so they don't grow up becoming selfish or possessive. Guide your children well and teach them the art of flexibility and forgiveness. This will mean their teenage years are much easier for them and you as well.

Romance, love and marriage

There's nothing fleeting about Taurus's approach to love. Taurean love is for keeps. When a Taurus opens his or her heart, your partner needs to understand that your devotion and intensity of love has to be reciprocated. There's nothing casual or fleeting in your approach.

Taurus needs to be assured that their partner's idea of love also includes companionship as part of the mix. Friendship is as important as the sexual joy of a relationship. Relationships are important to you but your concept of relating has to do with the durability of people and their interactions. Being a great friend, you'll go to any lengths to help someone in need. Your friends and family can always depend on you. You're proud of this fact.

The other key factor to your satisfaction in love is finding someone who will offer you the financial stability you seek. You like what money can buy and therefore your partner's ability to provide you with the necessities (and preferably the luxuries) of life are a measure of their love for you. Hopefully they won't see you as shallow when it comes to a relationship with you.

You're very persistent romantically and will therefore wait patiently until the right circumstances or person arrives on the scene. You're not at all prepared to settle for second best as you understand the problems that will arise from it. And, neither will you play second fiddle to anyone. If you feel as though you're being dated on the rebound, you'll soon put an end to it.

TAURUS

Your honesty is sometimes seen as ruthless by would-be suitors. Once these people get a taste of your single-mindedness they will realise that there's no mucking about with a Taurus. Making a commitment is a lifelong experience for you. They will need to raise their standards to a much higher level and must be prepared to offer you loyalty, fidelity and devotion.

You are possessive in some ways once you choose the person you consider to be a lifelong partner in love. You mustn't let people become objects, however. Love is an honourable thing and you need to offer your partner independence and freedom for their personal growth as well.

Once you find your soulmate, both of you must continue to improve your lives and evolve together. It might be easy for you to slip into a daily routine that is hard to break. Some Taureans become stagnant and stop romancing their mate once the thrill of the chase is over. You mustn't let this happen to you.

Try to remain youthful, playful and under all circumstances communicative about your feelings. As some Taureans get older they prefer to sweep their emotional problems under the rug and this only complicates things for them in their marriages. If you team up with someone who demonstrates their love for you and is sensitive to your needs you'll be more comfortable about sharing your deeper feelings with them. This will ensure your spiritual growth in the partnership.

Your sensual nature sometimes gets the better of you. You like to reward yourself with exciting and fun times for a job well done, but overindulgence needs to be checked so that you don't fall into the trap of excess in the pleasurable activities of eating, drinking and sensualising. Try to team up with someone who will balance these elements of your nature if you are prone to overdoing it.

THE TAURUS IDENTITY

Try not to live in the past too much and don't expect others to understand how you feel without letting them know what is on your mind. Get away from the rat-race on a regular basis and reconnect with nature. This is one way in which you, Taurus, will re-establish contact with your deeper, emotional self. This will go a long way towards keeping your love life fresh and vital.

Health, wellbeing and diet

Taurus is a physically strong sign. Nothing keeps you down for long even if you don't feel well from time to time. Your mental strength is just as strong, therefore your willpower carries you across the line making you robust, healthy and generally in an up-beat state of wellbeing.

Feeling well is not difficult for your star sign but overindulging in fine food and alcohol may eventually undermine your health. The three key words for Taurus in this regard are moderation, moderation and moderation.

Taurus does have a tendency to gain weight, especially later in life, so it's probably best to get into the habit of calorie counting earlier rather than later. It won't be too hard if you get into the swing of things when young and try not to eat too many sweets.

Most European languages originally sprang from Sanskrit or the Vedic language of India. It's not a well-known fact but the ancient Vedic astrological term for Venus is *Shukra*. This is the equivalent word for sugar. Taurus, being ruled by Venus, is very partial to sweets. Try to control your sweet tooth and it will ensure better health for you!

Taurus rules the throat, mouth, neck and face and therefore these parts of your body will trouble you from time to time. Your tonsils, thyroid, parathyroid, and upper spinal vertebrae as well as your jaw and mouth are also constitutionally weak. If

TAURUS

your thyroid happens to be causing trouble you'll feel very tired and lethargic.

Be strict with your dental hygiene and eat simple and easily digestible meals. This will protect you against some of the above health problems. Rich, sweet foods appeal to you so you need to avoid dietary indiscretions otherwise you'll gain weight.

Generally, most foods are good for you as long as you chew slowly and don't overeat. Also, eat additional amounts of fruit to aid your digestion.

Work

You love to work, Taurus. It's part of your basic make-up. You like the fact that money and wealth are a measure of the good work that you do. So, when asked to perform a task, you're attentive and efficient in fulfilling your obligations and are also very honest and punctual when it comes to meeting your appointments and deadlines.

The training of a Taurus takes a little longer but once they've learned the art or technique they can execute the job more effectively than anyone else.

You're a reliable worker and never, ever compromise the outcome by slacking off or doing the job half-heartedly. If you have the opportunity to handle money in your workplace, you are also very dependable in that respect. You treat your boss's money as if it's your own and never waste it.

You don't rush a business or commercial decision and your intuitive nature serves you well when conducting yourself in one on one transactions.

As long as ideas have a practical value you're happy to put your energy and time into them but, by the same token, if these concepts are airy-fairy without any practical plan or objective, you're hardly interested.

THE TAURUS IDENTITY

On the whole the best occupations for you are those that are practical and may include home sciences, gardening and landscape design. Taurus has an affinity with banking so a financial career is also excellent for you. Interior design, architecture, fashion or retail may attract you as well. Many Taureans are great in the make-up or hair styling industry as this is ruled by Venus.

Your lucky days

Your luckiest days are Friday, Wednesday and Saturday.

Your lucky numbers

Remember that the forecasts given later in the book will help you optimise your chances of winning. Your lucky numbers are:

6, 15, 24, 33, 42, 51

5, 14, 23, 32, 41, 50

8, 17, 26, 35, 44, 53

Your destiny years

Your most important years are 6, 15, 24, 33, 42, 51, 60, 78 and 87.

TAURUS

Star Sign Compatibility

TAURUS

He was a dreamer, a thinker, a speculative philosopher ... or, as his wife would have it, an idiot.

—Douglas Adams

Romantic compatibility

How compatible are you with your current partner, lover or friend? Did you know that astrology can reveal a whole new level of understanding between people simply by looking at their star sign and that of their partner? In this chapter I'd like to share with you some special insights that will help you better appreciate the strengths and challenges using Sun sign compatibility.

The Sun reflects your drive, willpower and personality. The essential qualities of two star signs blend like two pure colours, producing an entirely new colour. Relationships, similarly, produce their own emotional colours when two people interact. The following is a general guide to your romantic prospects with others and how, by knowing the astrological 'colour' of each other, the art of love can help you create a masterpiece.

When reading the following I ask you to remember that no two star signs are ever *totally* incompatible. With effort and compromise, even the most 'difficult' astrological matches can work. Don't close your mind to the full range of life's possibilities! Learning about each other and ourselves is the most important facet of astrology.

Each star sign combination is followed by the elements of those star signs and the result of their combining. For instance, Aries is a fire sign and Aquarius is an air sign and this combination produces a lot of 'hot air'. Air feeds fire and fire warms air. In fact, fire requires air. However, not all air and fire combinations work. I have included information about the different birth periods within each star sign and this will throw even more light on your prospects for a fulfilling love life with any star sign you choose.

Good luck in your search for love and may the stars shine upon you in 2009!

Compatibility quick reference guide

Each of the twelve star signs has a greater or lesser affinity with each other. Here's a quick reference guide on page 30 to who's hot and who's not so hot as far as your relationships are concerned.

TAURUS + ARIES
Earth + Fire = Lava

I remember many years ago a philosophical mind riddle that talked about an unstoppable force hitting an immovable object. Remember that? Looking back I now wonder if they were talking about the combination of Taurus and Aries.

As you know, you are immovable when you want to be: stubborn, and relentless when you believe your position to be true. Aries on the other hand has an incredibly fiery and powerful drive that challenges your position, being at a steadier and slower pace.

Aries is spontaneous in most areas of life but particularly where money is concerned this will present a problem for you in the long term. You're practical and conservative and very, very security conscious. You'll need to spend time re-educating Aries about their attitude in these areas.

Both of you like to be in control but in slightly different ways. You have a less obvious way of directing things than Aries. You will see them as being impulsive whereas you like to consider each and every aspect of a problem carefully before coming to a decision.

TAURUS

Quick reference guide: Horoscope compatibility between signs (percentage)

	Aries	Taurus	Gemini	Cancer	Leo	Virgo	Libra	Scorpio	Sagittarius	Capricorn	Aquarius	Pisces
Aries	60	65	65	65	90	45	70	80	90	50	55	65
Taurus	60	70	70	80	70	90	75	85	50	95	80	85
Gemini	70	70	75	60	80	75	90	60	75	50	90	50
Cancer	65	80	60	75	70	75	60	95	55	45	90	75
Leo	90	70	80	70	85	75	65	75	95	45	70	90
Virgo	45	90	75	75	75	70	80	85	70	95	50	75
Libra	70	75	90	60	65	80	80	85	80	85	50	70
Scorpio	80	85	60	95	75	85	85	90	80	65	95	50
Sagittarius	90	50	75	55	95	70	80	85	85	55	60	95
Capricorn	50	95	50	45	45	95	85	65	55	85	60	75
Aquarius	55	80	90	70	70	50	95	60	60	70	80	85
Pisces	65	85	50	90	75	70	50	95	75	85	55	80

STAR SIGN COMPATIBILITY

Aries likes to feel as if it knows best, and this will cause an unending battle of wills if you get drawn into taking the bait. It might seem that what I'm saying is all doom and gloom, but not necessarily. Although there are some striking differences between this star sign combination, it is surprising that I have personally observed several very successful Taurus–Aries duos.

Because Venus and Mars are your rulers, respectively, your sexual rapport is reasonably strong. Mars rules the dominant male energy and Venus the sensual and feminine. You will be attracted to the passion in the highly motivated Aries and they will in turn be drawn to your sensitive and nurturing qualities. I see you enjoying each other's company intimately.

Emotionally you are quite possessive whereas Aries likes to play the field. Loyalty is very powerful in the Taurus nature and this is one area that needs to be knotted out before either of you move forward in a long-term partnership. If you can make some concessions for these differences in each other's personalities, there's every possibility that the partnership will work out to be one of the better combinations of the zodiac.

If you find yourself drawn to Aries born between 21 and 29 March there could be problems financially. You don't want to end up carrying the burden of their financial mismanagement. You need someone who is more responsible with the dollars and cents.

I see exceptionally good relationships with Aries born between 30 March and 10 April, mainly because Leo also has an influence on them. This will affect the domestic satisfaction and thus promises to be a very good match. With these Aries being extremely charming, it is going to be hard for you not to be attracted to them.

Those Aries born between 11 and 20 April will be a little too wild and ambitious for your temperament. You like someone a little more down to earth than this.

TAURUS + TAURUS
Earth + Earth = Solid ground

Have you ever seen two bulls locking horns? Well, that's what's likely if you decide to entangle your emotional life with another Taurean. Let's talk about the emotional aspects first.

Both of you are very straightforward but have a tendency to hold your ground where your opinions are concerned. There's no beating around the bush, so even if your Taurus mate annoys you, you at least know what their position is (fixed, right?)

This is not to say that the double-Taurus combination can't work, it's just that beyond the soft, loving and sensual aspects of your nature, the day-to-day affairs of life will need to be dealt with. Sure, you can share affection and will certainly understand each other's needs, but you'll both be on the path of learning the art of flexibility as part of your life lesson together.

You like things to be in good taste and your Taurus partner will be able to provide you with all the finer things in life, knowing exactly how you feel and what is your heart's desire.

It's likely that when you first meet it will be in some arena in which Venus, your ruler, has influence; for example, a musical or artistic or social event. Venus also rules parties and fun places of amusement, so any of these areas is likely to draw you together if you're destined to become soulmates.

Both of you are very social creatures so expect many activities and fun outings together that will stimulate both of you. As a couple you'll be keen to make many new friends and this will be an important component of your relationship.

Because neither of you likes to change too easily, it will be difficult for this relationship to grow spiritually. One of you will need to be the initiator so that your time together will help you

STAR SIGN COMPATIBILITY

both develop as people. There is a strong level of complacency and, might I even say in the extreme, laziness, which is possible with a double-Taurus match.

You both need security, buckets of money and a safe haven, and these you can and will provide to each other. Don't let your individual work regimes intrude on your personal lives. This could be another reason for the relationship bogging down and not reaching its full potential. Usually, though, a Taurus and Taurus combination brings with it the promise of a happy home life, strong domestic bonds and long-term financial and emotional security.

If you are looking for the perfect Taurean as your partner, look no further than those born between 21 and 29 April. You will certainly feel a deep bond with them and this partnership will go far.

With Taurus individuals born between 30 April and 10 May I can see loads of romance and fun-filled times. Your sexual intimacy will be one of the notable highs of a relationship with them.

With Taureans born between 11 and 21 May I see a really great working relationship that will satisfy your financial needs, but it might not be enough to give you the lifelong emotional fulfilment you need.

TAURUS + GEMINI
Earth + Air = Dust

Venus your ruler and Mercury the ruler of Gemini are considered friendly planets in the scheme of astrology. This doesn't mean that there aren't significant differences in your style but it does essentially show that the two of you can get on quite well.

I rarely fail to see a Taurus who isn't slow and plodding in nature. This is how you like to approach your life and your

TAURUS

communication also follows this same pattern. Unlike you, your Gemini partner will prefer a great deal of variety and is sometimes a little too quick in drawing their conclusions. You see this as a type of immaturity, if the truth be known.

It doesn't mean you're not attracted to Gemini, however, as one of their key endearing qualities is their great sense of humour. Their conversational style is very alluring to you and, to your way of seeing things, if they could just slow the pace somewhat you'd have absolutely no doubt about giving this relationship your stamp of approval.

You always have many things to talk about and will spend a lot of time enjoying each other's company. Gemini will stimulate you to try new things and although this will be hard initially, you'll soon get a taste for it and enjoy it immensely. In the first stages you'll wonder how anyone can possibly do so much! Gemini, when controlled and self-directed, has a unique ability for achievement.

Some astrologers harp on too much about the frivolous and scattered energies of Gemini and maybe I'm a little guilty of that myself. But, if the truth be known, they are the most versatile of people and personally I love a good conversation with an excited and intelligent Gemini. I've no doubt that you too will be taken by them, Taurus.

I see much mutual pleasure between you, and sexually Gemini will take the lead. They have curious minds and like to explore so this will help take you out of your comfort zone to a new level of pleasure and sensual enjoyment.

Geminis born between 2 and 12 June are really well suited to you because your own ruling planet Venus holds sway over them. As well as being extremely intelligent and conversational, they also possess great aesthetic and cultural taste.

There is another class of Geminis born between 13 and 21 June and, if you choose to team up with them, you should expect life to be quite exciting, if not hectic. If you're a typical Taurean and like to maintain a fixed routine, these Geminis will most probably challenge you as they are very spontaneous in the way they live life.

Geminis born between 22 May and 1 June will get on well with you and offer you a different sort of lifestyle to which you are accustomed. As a typical Gemini, you can expect long and entertaining chats with them, which is attractive to you.

TAURUS + CANCER
Earth + Water = Mud

It's only natural for you to search for someone who is sensitive and who will in turn care for and nurture you in a relationship. This reflects your own emotional character. For this reason you needn't look any further than the lunar-ruled Cancer to satisfy you on this level.

Both of you are affectionate and Cancer will instinctively understand your needs. Cancer is also moody, being ruled by the changeable Moon, but your solid and steadfast personality is one of the few zodiac signs that can easily handle this.

I see great friendship and satisfaction socially for both of you, and you will be able to draw Cancer out into a more sociable type of arena due to your Venus-ruled sign. Once they get a taste for good company there's no stopping them.

Taurus is very practical while Cancer is domestic and family oriented. This is a great combination for family life and brings you both an immense of satisfaction if the relationship happens to click and go the distance. You will be extremely supportive of each other in a family environment.

Cancer is an emotional water sign, which also brings with it considerable spirituality and psychic ability. You will find

TAURUS

yourself drawn to the deeper mysteries of life in your relationship with a Cancer and will progress not only materially but also spiritually.

This relationship has some elements of excitement and sexual attraction. Both star signs are ruled by feminine planets, which show you are both perceptive to each other's emotional as well as physical needs.

Compassion and empathy are also strong points in this relationship so you'll both be keen to satisfy each other in every respect without being asked. There is a good intuitive connection and feel for each other in this match. You'll enjoy those moments of mind reading where you don't even have to say a thing to understand exactly what you both mean. That's pretty rare, isn't it?

Generally Taurus and Cancer are quite compatible, but a relationship with Cancerians born between 22 June and 3 July is even better. I see a sensitive and loving match between the two of you. However, one of you will have to play the hero if the relationship starts to 'wash out' with sentimentality. This combination needs some added strength, and that will more than likely come from you, Taurus.

You are very attracted to Cancerians who are born between 4 and 13 July. These people are co-ruled by Mars, which is your marital planet. Obviously a relationship with someone born during this cycle should grow into something special and would be a good marriage combination.

If you have your eye on a Cancer born between 14 and 23 July, friendship is more ideally suited to you both rather than any deep, sexual relationship. Although you'll have a strong attraction for each other there will be something lacking and for you that sexual aspect is essential if you are to feel comfortable.

STAR SIGN COMPATIBILITY

TAURUS + LEO
Earth + Fire = Lava

A match between Venus ruled Taurus and Sun ruled Leo can be a pretty eye-catching combination, if you ask me. An elemental mix of earth and fire is really hot rocks and lava, as the heading indicates. You'll both be attracted to each other, of course, but there's more than one type of a heat in a relationship and therefore your energies will need to be managed carefully if you're to experience anything other than a sexually sizzling time together.

Your Leo friend is larger than life and likes to be in the spotlight, whereas you prefer to take the back seat in the partnership. You will love the vitality, warmth and social gregariousness that go with the Leo personality. In fact, it's as if they're constantly performing on the stage of life and this will fascinate and entertain you.

If you do decide to share your feelings with Leo it will have to be a two-way street. They will want you to reciprocate and direct some of that warmth and vitality to them. They are somewhat self-centred at times. One thing that will comfort you, however, is the loyalty of Leo. They are protective of family and loved ones and are committed to providing for their pride. This is reflected in their home life so they will offer you the security you need, don't worry about that.

As I said earlier, physically Leo has a way of putting you in touch with your deeper sexual feelings. You might feel overpowered by the magnetic quality of Leo and will need to set your own pace if you initially feel uncomfortable about moving too fast into the highly charged zone of love with them.

I strongly recommend you take things one step at a time and don't let your primal instincts overshadow your practical considerations in this relationship, as pleasurable as it is.

TAURUS

Leos born between 24 July and 4 August have much in common with you and make great partners. You both like the idea of family and a soft place to land in the family sense. These Leo-born individuals will protect and nurture you and you will feel comfortable in your support for them in everything they do.

With Leos born between 14 and 23 August I see much passion added to an already general compatibility between you. Mars dominates them and this will at times create some turbulent episodes. Relationships for you need to be a two-way street and you will find these individuals taking more than they give.

Take some precautions with those born between 5 and 13 August. We all know how money and security conscious Taurus is and there's nothing worse for you than unnecessary risks. These people will be spendthrifts who make you feel quite uncomfortable on a material level. But, they do come up with some amazing concepts for business and, if you are prepared for the odd gamble, their wacky schemes might just pay off, to your and their satisfaction.

TAURUS + VIRGO
Earth + Earth = Solid ground

There are rare combinations astrologically that are nearly perfect and the Taurus–Virgo match is one of them. The reason for this is that each different star sign is categorised elementally and in this case each of you happens to be an earth sign. Virgo will complement you perfectly on many levels and you should feel naturally attracted to each other.

You'll find much of yourself reflected in Virgo's practical, no-nonsense approach to life. They're down to earth and fully aware of what needs to be done on a day-to-day basis. This will instil confidence in you that your Virgo partner will support your financial needs and future material security.

STAR SIGN COMPATIBILITY

You must understand that Virgo does have a reputation for being somewhat of a perfectionist. They have very high standards and can at times be quite critical of others, even of themselves. Dealing with their habit of mentally nitpicking this, that and the other will be a challenge for you from time to time.

Virgo is ruled by Mercury and is therefore an excellent communicator. You'll need to be patient when discussing certain issues with them as they don't exactly travel directly from A to B in their sentences. You might feel a little overpowered by their intellectual gymnastics.

Virgo reacts strongly and is often hypersensitive. You must be careful how you criticise them (even though they are the master critics). They are very thin-skinned and so tread carefully before you openly hammer them, especially in public.

Art, fashion, music and even cooking would be activities you'd mutually share and enjoy. You need to give Virgo ample opportunity to relax as they have busy minds and nature or outdoor activities will work wonders for them.

Virgo is romantic and tends to stimulate your passions; therefore this match is sure to work for you. Your affinity on this one level will more than compensate for any other shortcomings in the relationship.

All Virgos are attractive to you and they will feel the same. Those born between 14 and 23 September, however, better reflect your life ideals and your personal desires. There's a strong karmic and spiritual connection with these people and you will feel you've known them before (possibly in another life?).

Virgos born between 24 August and 2 September are very playful, sensual and sexual in nature. You feel very comfortable with them and therefore believe your relationship will be straightforward and honest without too many barriers between you.

TAURUS

Virgos born between 3 and 13 September have a serious side to their nature. They are very highly strung and volatile individuals and therefore you need to be a happy-go-lucky sort of Taurean if this relationship has a chance of survival.

TAURUS + LIBRA
Earth + Air = Dust

Both of you are ruled by sensual Venus so it's hardly surprising that you'll be attracted to these interesting characters.

Libra is an air sign, which relates to the intellectual qualities within all of us. Earth relates to material instincts, which are your specific talent. This is good as you'll be able to ground the sometimes scattered energies of Libra.

Both of you are social creatures and will enjoy plenty of fun times together; but you should tell Libra at the outset that you don't want this to be at the expense of your domestic stability. Social life versus domestic life could end up being one of the key issues that need working on. A reasonable approach will be necessary so that both of you are satisfied in this partnership.

Librans are extremely sensitive and intelligent people and often have a strong social conscience. Librans will instinctively know how to deal with you even in your most stubborn moments. You'd be surprised but on the other hand a little annoyed as you feel they have some sort of subtle control over you.

Libra understands your security needs, but do you understand their intellectual needs? Everything hinges on that question. If you have a Libran partner who is a sensitive and co-operative individual, I see this relationship being first class. You'll nurture and support each other perfectly.

Libra will help you in work-related areas as well. You must, however, be prepared to listen to their ideas, of which there is

STAR SIGN COMPATIBILITY

no shortage. Libra can propel you forward towards your goals but you mustn't let your ego believe you know more than they do all the time.

Libra will revitalise you and, if the best of both of you is brought to the table, you'll feel physically great as well as emotionally happy in each other's company. However, if your emotions are withheld, this will impact adversely on your physical wellbeing.

There are some key factors in your romantic association with Libra. An important one is related to your lifestyle adjustments and finding a happy medium. You must accommodate each other and not do it simply out of a sense of pleasing the other. Even your sexual relationship will not be able to counteract any dissatisfaction that arises in your life paths if they become parallel railway tracks.

Those Librans born between 24 September and 3 October are doubly ruled by Venus and their life goals will be very much in tune with yours. Your relationship with them looks set to be a beauty because you're so connected to each other.

Librans born between 4 and 13 October are also associated with Uranus and Aquarius and therefore have very fast-moving minds, which are sometimes a little off-beat as well. You could feel unstable or even insecure with them and will need time to think this one through a little more.

Librans born between 14 and 23 October are extremely attracted to you. They have sensuality oozing from every pore of their skin. You'll be attracted to this sensuality and could have a very powerful relationship. Over and above your physical attraction to each other, communication will be strong and your own social skills will definitely need to be honed to keep up with them.

TAURUS + SCORPIO
Earth + Water = Mud

Here again we see opposite signs of the zodiac powerfully attracted to each other, with Taurus and the Mars–Pluto-driven Scorpio being a natural fit together, temperamentally. There doesn't seem to be any denying this. Mind you, not all opposite signs of the zodiac are as compatible, but Taurus–Scorpio can make a reasonable go of it.

The deep and penetrating eyes of Scorpio will overwhelm you and possibly confuse you on your first meeting. You'll feel an intense passion for them and even when they're not around you'll find it hard to concentrate on anything but them. Scorpio will feel the same way because Mars and Venus have an undeniable connection with each other.

Both of you are fixed signs and therefore stubbornness will be a trait you both need to overcome if only to make this wonderful relationship of yours easier to endure. The question is, do you want to be right, or do you want to enjoy this relationship? Very often Scorpio and Taurus are engaged in a battle of wills.

Scorpio needs to express their deeper feelings of sexuality and this will bolster your ego initially but sooner or later you'll need to know and feel a deeper emotional connection with them if this relationship is to develop into something fully satisfying for you. Of course, physical closeness is important to you but you want more.

Scorpio is the most sexual of the star signs and Taurus is not too badly endowed with this quality, either. Therefore, this is a very powerful and enduring combination but will also bring with it formidable challenges, not only emotionally but financially. You also need to work out who is going to rule the roost economically. Talk with your Scorpio mate about these things if you're serious about a relationship with them. Even if they don't say as much as you'd like, they'll be taking every word you speak to heart.

Many Scorpios get on extremely well with you but those born between 24 October and 2 November are even better suited as far as I see. You are compatible emotionally, mentally, sexually and most importantly, spiritually. You can safely make long-term plans and commit yourself to them.

Scorpios born between 3 and 12 November are better suited to you as friends rather than lovers. You do, however, have good spiritual and karmic bonds with them and I anticipate some unusual and memorable experiences for the two of you. These Scorpios spin beautiful dreams, which may enamour you but be a little too impractical for your Taurean commonsense.

If you're considering a Scorpio born between 13 and 22 November, you mustn't expect anything other than moderately compatible results. They are extremely sensitive individuals whose moods shift like the tides. If you prefer emotionally stable partners they may not be the ones to offer it to you.

TAURUS + SAGITTARIUS
Earth + Fire = Lava

The two of you are both pretty different types of characters with you, Taurus, being primarily concerned with the real world: a world you can touch, feel and see. Your Sagittarian partner has a very different philosophy to you and values freedom, independence and spontaneity in all forms.

Because of this it's not a particularly natural combination because Sagittarius doesn't offer you the rock-solid security you're after. You happen to be a creature of habit, whereas from time to time, Sagittarius throws all care to the wind preferring to live by their wits. Sagittarius is also brutally

TAURUS

honest, direct and often blunt in the way they express themselves. This can be shocking to you at first but secretly you like the fact they're honest and see this as a crude form of integrity.

Sagittarius is a mutable or common sign. This means they are malleable, like putty, and can more easily adapt to the flow of life than you. There may be some valuable lessons for the fixed sign of Taurus in a meeting with them, don't you think?

Whereas you find it hard to change or let go of the past that easily, Sagittarians seem to adapt so easily to life that this can be scary. They love change, exploration and discovering new things, places and unusual people. If your choice is to go along for the ride with them, expect to be shaken to the very foundations of your Taurean self.

There are many pluses on the sexual side, however, because your ruling planets Venus and Jupiter are a lucky duo. You see, Jupiter is a spiritual planet and does endow your Sagittarian friend with a deeper understanding of life and empathy. You'll be drawn to this and realise that beneath the surface of the Sagittarian bravado is a gem of a person.

If you're looking for a soulmate within the Sagittarian ranks, you needn't look any further than those born between 2 and 11 December. Also being influenced by Aries and Mars you are likely to share some wild and exciting times with them. Mars does, however, make them antagonistic and impulsive. This can be overwhelming as it impacts upon their ability to save money and this is something that will unnerve you.

Those born between 12 and 22 December bring with them lots of fun, humour and camaraderie. You'll have a great time with them and will be seen as an attractive couple. Nightclubbing and mixing with mutual friends will underpin your relationship. These Sagittarians will look after you and are not afraid to show their appreciation.

STAR SIGN COMPATIBILITY

Take care with Sagittarians born between 23 November and 1 December because your luck will be adversely affected by them. Money is a problem for them if they don't respect it. If you do find yourself in a relationship, you need to be clear about where you stand on money matters. Don't let money come between you.

TAURUS + CAPRICORN
Earth + Earth = Solid ground

Capricorn is attractive to your earthy and practical nature. There's nothing airy-fairy about Capricorn and therefore you feel an immediate respect for them when you meet them. Both of you being earth signs indicates a natural affinity for each other.

Each of you is traditional, with Capricorn being even more conservative than you. More than any other sign, Capricorn will make you feel secure and their ambitions seem to have a practical, no-nonsense quality about them. This is something that very much appeals to you.

You like the way Capricorn expresses their love for you by supporting you with a lifestyle that makes you feel comfortable, that you can grow with them and achieve even greater things.

But Capricorn is also changeable and they like to try new things so occasionally this will push your boundaries beyond that of cold comfort. You must be open enough to let Capricorn lead you in this sense because it can only help you grow and feel closer to them.

Sexually Taurus is needier than Capricorn, which is a more withdrawn and less expressive sign. This of course is a superficial and very generalised description of them and you mustn't let your first impressions deter you from exploring the deeper, sensual part of the Capricorn personality. The two of you have

TAURUS

much in common and will experience fulfilment on an intimate level as well.

Capricorns born between 2 and 10 January are really compatible with you. This is because they are co-ruled by your ruling planet, Venus. These individuals are not as insular as the typical Capricorn and will also be surprisingly sensual. Venus makes them more demonstrative, which is ideal for what you're looking for. The two of you have a strong unspoken bond and this is a relationship that can endure.

Capricorns born between 23 December and 1 January are also compatible with you. If you're interested in finance and material security, they'll offer it to you. They are extremely hard workers and will provide for you and the family, not just in the essentials of life but the luxuries as well. Your professional and financial goals are in keeping with each other.

A fine relationship can be expected with those born between 11 and 20 January. This too can be a perfect love match as they are quite romantic individuals. They know how to win your heart and this is due to Mercury's influence. There is a touch of Virgo in them which adds perfection to their style but also, don't forget, as with most Virgos, a touch of criticism as well.

TAURUS + AQUARIUS
Earth + Air = Dust

Taurus, you're extremely conservative, practical and matter-of-fact in everything you do. You need to know where things are and, when Aquarius lobs into your scene, the contrast will be quite stark as they are far more progressive and ideological than you.

You'd like to feel as though you could move forward with an Aquarian partner but the question is how much challenge

STAR SIGN COMPATIBILITY

can you endure? They will seem far too impractical for your taste. And, likewise, you will frustrate them because you need a little extra time before stepping out of your comfort zone.

Aquarius is broad-based in its views, which encompasses social issues, politics and other community affairs, whereas you're more focused on tangible and immediate interests. You believe that family, a circle of friends and your loved ones are where your attention should be focused. The concept of humanity being regarded as your larger family will take time to warm to, unlike Aquarius. So again, there are significant differences in what you feel should be your focus of attention.

Both Taurus and Aquarius are fixed signs so there doesn't seem too much scope for either of you to adjust your opinions. Being both creatures of habit you will stick to your guns and this will be more pronounced as you both get older.

Aquarius is no respecter of convention and this also seems to be the case between the sheets. You'll need to trust them when they take you on their sensual explorations because sex is more than just an emotional day-to-day habitual process for them.

They want major discoveries in the process of love, so your open mind is as important as your willing body to them. It may be that the relationship with Aquarius is better suited to you on a casual basis rather than a long-term committed relationship.

Be careful of Aquarians born between 21 and 30 January. This is an unstable combination and you won't feel at all comfortable with their abrupt and avante garde routine. There's an alternative astrological joke that alludes to the fact that Aquarians are sometimes at the heart of revolutions and political overthrows. Even if they aren't necessarily political, they will voice their opinions strongly, I can assure you.

TAURUS

You do, however, have a pretty good connection with those Aquarians born between 31 January and 8 February. Mercury is a lucky planet for you and has a certain co-rulership over them. They have quick minds, a good sense of fun, and you are both therefore well suited.

Aquarians born between 9 and 19 February have the touch of Venus and Libra and therefore reflect some of your Taurean qualities. This is a reasonably good match astrologically, but you will find it hard to deal with their changeable minds. Notwithstanding this, the future with these individuals could be quite rosy.

TAURUS + PISCES
Earth + Water = Mud

Friendship seems to be the operative word when we talk about a combination between Taurus and Pisces. Social life and mixing with friends will be a common thread for both of you. More importantly, developing mateship and companionship between you will be a lifelong pleasure. Once all the physical attraction and sexual excitement has quietened down, it's nice to know that both of you will still feel very comfortable with each other.

Pisces is a very sensitive and idealistic sign and therefore your practical nature will sometimes be at odds with this idealistic mate. Pisces will point to the stars and ask you to see beyond your practical affairs and your material desires and goals and to put your faith in a higher power. They'll have to prove they can weigh the scales of spirituality and humanitarianism with down-to-earth practicality if their opinion is to be worthwhile, in your estimation.

You on the other hand are firmly planted on Earth and demand that Pisces get real and forget about their out-of-this-world visions and empty dreams. Both of you are right and

STAR SIGN COMPATIBILITY

both of you are wrong! The truth is that you need to counterbalance each other in this relationship and take the best from each other's personalities to grow in yourselves.

You needn't be black and white all the time and in this way you can absorb some of the spiritual knowledge that Pisces brings to the relationship. Be gentle in your approach to Pisces as well. Show them the benefits of practical, routine day-to-day existence. They secretly want to be anchored and you may just be the one to show them how.

Taurus and Pisces do attract each other and that's because you are both feminine, receptive signs of the zodiac. Your emotions are strong and your feelings will resonate well with each other. Your sexual compatibility is based upon your emotional fulfilment of each other. This is the starting point for a satisfactory sexual connection.

I see the potential for a great meeting of the hearts and minds with those born between 20 and 28 or 29 February. However, these individuals are truly visionary and see the world from another level, so you might find these people far too impracticable to sustain a long-term relationship.

Pisces born between 1 and 10 March are not really that compatible with you but they are responsive and emotional so it might be worth giving them a try. Teach them strength and decisiveness and don't dismiss them because they haven't developed these qualities to the same level as you. Practicality is a learned technique. Be their teacher.

Mars and Pluto dominate Pisceans born between 11 and 20 March and this makes them powerful and intense individuals. They are seductive and exciting to be with as well as extraordinarily sexual, as you'll soon learn. These are the strong, silent types and will be more demanding than you're prepared to accept. Unless you make some serious compromises you will not want to pursue a relationship with this type of Piscean.

TAURUS

2009:
The Year Ahead

TAURUS

Fortune favours the brave.

—Publius Terence

Romance and friendship

An old mentor of mine once told me that what is good is not always necessarily pleasant. As far as your relationships are concerned, we could well apply this maxim to your romantic life because the first part of the year might seem serious and a little less than exciting.

This is due to the challenging relationship between your ruling planets Venus and Saturn. The effects of this will be particularly strong in the latter part of January and this means you'll be reappraising long-term relationships.

If you can get through these initial hurdles, you'll be well along the way to seeing an improvement in your love life, but only if you're prepared to talk and release any grudges or ill-feelings you have towards your partner.

Up till the 3rd of February, it would be a good idea to take time out to think through what it is you want and don't want in your personal life. If you distract yourself too much with parties, outings and other social activities, you won't really get to the bottom of your issues.

There is considerable help for you due to the beneficial rays of Jupiter and this means you can climb the social ladder of success, have a great time and meet many interesting people. It also means your honesty will pay very handsome dividends in smoothing over your relationships.

Venus moves to your Sun sign in the early part of February, so make sure the first impressions you give are your best as this is how people will remember you. You could also raise the benchmark when it comes to your love life. If your partner or, for that matter any newcomer on the scene, is not acting in accordance with what you think are the appropriate rules of play, say something about it. Don't put up with anything less than you feel you deserve.

By the end of March you will feel powerful and in your own element due to the favourable vibrations of the Sun. You definitely get a boost mentally, emotionally and physically. I see that you'll be able to remove many of your stresses and this is a great time to organise yourself socially, to get out into the limelight and feel as though you're living life to the fullest. Because the full Moon at this time occupies an area relating to your health, you need to be modest in the way you party as you may tend to live a little too hard during this cycle.

Your ruling planet Venus moves in reverse motion throughout the period of late March and April and this means you'll have to backtrack over old ground, particularly in areas of love and romance. For some born under Taurus, an unhappy relationship that ended may still be lurking in the shadows and unfinished emotional business needs to be attended to. Uncomfortable communications need to be addressed, as hard as that may be. Try not to do anything underhanded or be vengeful when others try to be sneaky or undermine you. It will be hard but don't lower your standards.

Passion can once again be strong and very inviting throughout May when Venus and Mars do their attractive dance together in the heavens. This will stimulate you to explore new territory socially and sexually. This is an excellent period for lovers to investigate and reignite the flames of their passion, if the fire has been waning.

The full Moon in May and also in June reveals much about your sexual activities and intimacy with your partner. In June, if you're feeling inhibited and uncomfortable with some aspects of your personality or physical appearance, you'll need to dig deeper into your arsenal of psychological insights to lift your ball game to extract the most out of your partnerships.

TAURUS

In July Mars and Venus continue their association only this time in your Sun sign. If you've been standing on the sidelines waiting for love to knock at your door, you may become impatient now and opt to take the more aggressive stance in demanding what you feel you deserve. You'll be looking great by the 12th, so don't for a minute think that your attractiveness won't work magic: it will. Don't forget, though, that astrology is all about karmic influences and timing. Time your entrances and exits this year.

The new Moon on the 22nd says that you'll be devising new communication techniques, especially if you previously haven't had the results you'd like. Journeys, travel to unusual places and social activities that are associated with learning and communication are excellent ways of increasing your chances at love in 2009.

Between July and September it's up to you to get out there and make it happen. There's no way you'll have the chance of meeting your soulmate by sitting on the sidelines or behind closed doors.

And, speaking of closed doors, the period of August is a time when you'll naturally want to vegetate and spend more time in the comfort of your own home; but you must resist this, even if you do have additional responsibilities with family members. Try to organise yourself early in the month, which will leave the latter half of August free for you to set up some important engagements throughout September.

Your love affairs will reach a pinnacle in September and, especially up to the 18th, you could be completely besotted. I would suggest that you take things slowly because the close proximity to Saturn could dampen your initial enthusiasm when you learn some deeper truths about a person.

At this time, love is not artificial but it does involve accepting another person with their faults and, at this point, some

2009: THE YEAR AHEAD

additional baggage from the past. Are you up to the task, Taurus? You may have to take additional responsibility for this person in some way further down the line if you don't go into the relationship with your eyes wide open.

As a parent, September will also draw you into some important negotiations with children. Helping them through some of their difficult situations could draw you away from the activities you'd prefer to be doing yourself. However, the action of the Sun and Saturn is indeed one that relates to shouldering those additional burdens and responsibilities of others as well.

Some of your newfound friendships will be so sudden that they'll spin your head. After October you are likely to again find yourself in the enviable position of meeting some very colourful characters, indeed. With Mercury and Venus moving through your zone of amusement, love affairs and creative enterprise, October will bolster your level of enthusiasm to an all-time high.

It's also worth mentioning that, with Jupiter continuing its journey through your zodiac sector of Aquarius, you will be sought after, not just for your fun value and friendship but for the wisdom and support you offer others. Your knowledge and your experience are coming to fruition and so this is the perfect blend of energies to draw life partners and karmic friends to you.

The Sun makes its important transit through your marital zone in November along with Mercury, and soon after with Venus. These three planets highlight the importance of the month for many Taureans. The cherry on the cake is the new Moon of the 16th, which is encouraging to you if your question is: 'Is this the right person for me?' The answer should be 'yes' and any new romantic venture should be extremely favourable for you.

TAURUS

Although your social life will continue to give you oodles of stimulation, the overriding influence seems to be one of clarification with your existing relationships, communicating your feelings and taking love to newfound heights. The continuing effect of Jupiter is such that you will not be interested in casual affairs but will want deeper meaning and longer lasting bonds.

It looks likely that in the closing chapter of 2009 you will indeed fulfil these desires. It will be important to note that Mars in its relationship with Jupiter can make you overeager and also exaggerative in your view and expectation of others. Remain realistic, don't demand too much from those you love and, likewise, offer good counsel and support to them. The year 2009 will certainly be one in which your romantic life and friendships will reveal a whole new level of meaning for you.

This is the start of even greater things as Jupiter positively influences your family life and domestic happiness. Remain confident, Taurus, because I see exciting and important developments for you romantically. If you're prepared to work with the planetary energies this will be certainly a year to remember.

Work and money

It's a rare occurrence to find the two lucky planets of Mercury and Jupiter affecting your career zone simultaneously. But that is precisely what happens at the outset of 2009 and this can only be seen as an extraordinarily lucky omen for you, work wise.

Throughout January take the bull by the horns and get the word out; don't be afraid to showcase your talents and advertise your skills. This is the time to let others know how capable you are and no doubt you will be received favourably and rewarded for so doing.

2009: THE YEAR AHEAD

A large number of planets assemble in the upper part of your horoscope as 2009 commences and this shows just how important your professional life will be this year.

The new Moon on the 26th tells us that you are ready for change and by February you may even find yourself in a new position or role with more money than you had expected. Events move rather quickly, suddenly, due to the new Moon being near Uranus, indicating sudden yet positive gains and profits to you.

Your finance planet Mercury is also well positioned to give you quick turnover and unusual sources of income throughout the year. Due to its influence on speculation, March is a perfect time to consider the stock market and any other sort of investment venture.

Let me suggest, however, that you get in and out quickly before April and then only after the second week of May return to the market if you choose to be riskier than normal. For Taureans who are steadier and less likely to take these unnerving gambles, the new Moon of the 24th of May should settle your affairs and bring more stability to your life. June also finds a new Moon in your finance zone, which indicates these two months will bring tremendous focus to money matters, security and other issues of long-term material interest.

The months of July and August are interesting inasmuch as your profit planets Jupiter and Neptune conjoin in your employment sector. There may be some confusion about your role and what you're supposed to do in work. For some of you, redundancies or dramatic shifts and shake-ups in your professional sphere could cause a few sleepless nights. Remain optimistic and under no circumstances let gossip and rumours determine your state of mind. If you have any concerns about your career security, get the answers straight from the horse's mouth: your boss.

TAURUS

Throughout September, don't be too impulsive with those whom you work. The challenging aspect of Mercury and Mars could cause conflicts with co-workers. You are also likely to say 'yes' quicker than your brain can process the requests you receive. This will cause later regret if you accept jobs and other responsibilities that you're not capable of fulfilling. Think ahead before giving the thumbs up.

Be careful of power struggles during September and October and, in every instance, make sure you're armed with the appropriate facts before going into battle. Your key word will be tenacity during the last few months of the year as Mars and Pluto shake up your communications and possibly even force you to reconsider a contractual obligation or two. If you happen to be on the receiving end of a contract or agreement, dedicate extra time to looking at the fine print before signing off.

In November, when Mercury and the Sun enter your public relations zone, you can develop your business contacts and associations that will hold you in good stead. Even if you don't happen to be professional as such, this is a lucky period in which the connections you make will somehow bring you financial benefits at some point in time. Don't be dismissive of those you come in contact with because all that glitters is not gold. Occasionally you meet someone who is fantastic at first sight, but time reveals another side to them.

Much of this comes to a head by the new Moon of the 16th. In this last part of the year there are indicators for a strong drive for property transactions due to the placement of Mars in your domestic sphere. You may want to roll up your sleeves, renovate to improve the value of your house or place of dwelling, or simply get at that overdue gardening.

Finally, with the closure of 2009, Mercury, your income planet, finishes its journey in the eighth and ninth zones of your horoscope. Your shared finances will need to be looked at carefully and, if you're dissatisfied with the arrangement, you should make the appropriate changes. Your ninth zone relates to legal matters and this may be a key to making the coming year or two more profitable for you. You mustn't accept anything that is less than a win–win situation for all concerned.

Karma, luck and meditation

This is indeed an important year for you romantically, owing to the powerful gathering of planets in your ninth zone of past karma. Pluto, Mars, the Sun, Jupiter and Mercury bring through to you an amazing number of opportunities, all of which may not be easily synchronised.

The key point here will be in making the right choices, whether or not the opportunities will present themselves to you. However, Mercury and Jupiter tell me that your awareness is acute and you're likely to seize upon the most profitable opportunities available this year.

Mercury is lucky for income and speculative ventures. Because it rules younger children and your future karma as well, there is something to be said for your association with younger people who can introduce you to a whole new vista of experiences; experiences that were probably not available to you before. Make sure you remain open-minded and open-hearted, especially in the first part of the year.

The north node, or karma force, is situated in your career zone throughout the first half of the year and then shifts in the very last few days of July to the area of long journeys, travels and again past karmic influences. Until then your desire and luck will be strongly focused on work and achieving the type of reputation that will ensure the steady and practically secure life any Taurean dreams about.

Venus as your ruling planet is also to be counted as a karmic and lucky planet for you and in the area of relationships

TAURUS

it will offer you some exciting potential between October and December. As I just mentioned, the secret of capitalising on these vibrant energies is to remain open and see what life has in store for you. From what I see in your horoscope, most of it will be fun and exceedingly fulfilling.

TAURUS

2009: Month by Month Predictions

JANUARY

I seldom end up where I wanted to go, but almost always end up where I need to be.

—Douglas Adams

Highlights of the month

The year 2009 is a really big year for Taurus and January is a great month from which to springboard into the coming cycle. It's an exciting period for you so get ready for a jam-packed life full of opportunities and new experiences.

I see plenty of planets and stars sparkling in the most fortuitous part of your horoscope. Therefore, success, social popularity and an increasing level of self-confidence is what I predict for you during this initial stage, if not most of the year.

Your moods will alternate between a desire for social activity and solitary moments of peace where you'd prefer just to get away from the rat-race. Your mind will feel much more steady after the 5th when the Moon enters its most powerful sign, your Sun sign, of Taurus. Your emotions will feel strong and controlled. This will certainly go a long way to giving you confidence in the way you deal with relationships.

2009: JANUARY

Firstly, you'll be reorienting your activities towards your home and domestic concerns, particularly up until the full Moon of the 11th. You may realise there's been considerable unfinished business in this area of your life and you'll have to make some choices between work demands and family members also requesting you to help them. Tie up many of these family 'loose ends'.

I see an immense uplifting in your energies between the 12th and the 15th, but you may also push yourself a little too hard at this time and by the 14th will start to feel some of your energy reserves dwindling. Do be careful at this time as you are likely to push yourself beyond your limits and find you need recovery time between the 16th and 17th.

Some born under Taurus will be a little confused about their symptoms and you can take this to be a signal that it is more than likely a nervous or stress complaint rather than anything physical in origin.

Relationships are favoured between the 15th and the 20th and, if you need to have serious discussions on matters of intimacy and romance, this is the time to do it. Things could get a little tough when Venus and Saturn enter into a difficult phase around the 24th—your or your partner's affections may dim just a little (but only for a while so don't overplay the effects).

A solar eclipse occurs on the 26th in your career zone. This signifies some important turning point for many Taureans and changes are definitely afoot. Don't sweep your dissatisfaction under the rug. Speak to your employer if something is eating away at you and causing you distress in your professional sphere. Get advice and don't worry about things that haven't yet happened. Be as practical as you can

Romance and friendship

If you feel obstructed in your efforts to improve yourself, be patient. Life has its own timetable and pushing it around only

TAURUS

delays the inevitable improvements of which you dream. A friend is instrumental in pointing you in the direction of a self-help 'guru' or psychology book between the 1st and the 5th.

A sudden urge to makeover your home brings out the creative 'interior designer' in you between the 11th and the 15th. Align your dreams with your budget and financial abilities, however, as expensive tastes will cost you more than money (peace of mind). Accept the advice of others in this initiative.

Your health and vitality will be an issue on the 16th and 17th. Don't let your psychosomatic fears make matters worse. If you're worried, get a check-up. The Moon is fast-moving so it's probably nothing. Keep yourself warm as well if you live in a cooler climate.

Rejection is hard to take but has its own lessons to teach you just now. Between the 15th and the 20th one door may close so be ready for a new one to open magically. Discussions with a friend at a distance will bring solace to your mind and help overcome a personal challenge.

Your admiration for a lover or partner is marred by their financial concerns on the 28th. You want to advise them on fiscal prudence but this might be unwise. Let them sort out their own financial mess and simply enjoy a romantic evening together.

On the 30th, if you have doubts about some aspect of your past you mustn't brush them away. Someone in your family arena has the answer to a long-standing problem but embarrassment could make it hard for you to ask the right questions. Overcome your fears and resolve the matter.

Work and money

Money matters need to be revisited on the 7th and 8th. You thought you had it worked out, didn't you? Well, an oversight will rear its ugly head just when you thought you had put the deal to bed. Get some good financial advice to secure the transaction if you need to.

Do you need an extension on a payment of your bank account or mortgage? Unfortunately you may need to speak to your bank about this between the 15th and 18th. You'll regret some of your financial behaviour but rest assured that the direction you'll take is correct and will eventually be seen as a good move to resolve these issues.

Over-emotionalism is a certain cause of confusion in life on the 21st. Numbers have to add up and, as beautiful as creative dreaming is, it doesn't pay the bills. Add and subtract ... ordinary maths procedures will show you the results in black and white. It's as simple as that!

Your creative business and professional ideas need appropriate company to appreciate their value on the 26th. If you're with a bunch of deaf people who aren't sensitive to your creative worth it's time to move on to greener pastures. A business event is socially beneficial to you.

Destiny dates

Positive: 1, 2, 3, 4, 5, 11, 12, 13, 14, 15, 17, 19, 20, 26

Negative: 7, 8, 15, 16, 17, 21, 24, 30

Mixed: 14, 16, 17, 18

FEBRUARY

Highlights of the month

During February you may throw all cares to the wind and prefer to opt for a life of ease and luxury. With the effervescent month of January behind you, you will certainly feel as if you deserve to reward yourself for an intense effort, but could find yourself swinging to the other extreme. Be careful not to waste valuable time on activities that don't produce results.

Balance your work and pleasure and remember, as the Buddha once said, 'The middle ground is the golden path.' In other words, be moderate even if you must have that luxury item that has been creating that desire for sometime.

It's likely that after the 3rd you'll find it reasonably difficult to resist spending money on some big-ticket item, even if you don't necessarily need it. This will be more than justified when good news in your work sphere brings with it an increased opportunity for additional income resulting in some spare cash.

At this same time your drive for professional success will dominate many of your activities, particularly over the next month or two and you'll be surprised at just how much you can achieve in such a short space of time.

This cycle is tense socially and friendships are in somewhat of a strange no-man's-land. Due to the push and pull influence of the two very different planets Uranus and Saturn, you will want some brand new changes in your social life but may be stuck in the past at the same time.

You will need to assess carefully the value of your relationships, and some hard decisions as to who should stay and who should go will be reached. The catalyst for this could be meeting someone new after the 9th and this could develop into a romantic relationship for those of you who are single. They could open your eyes to a whole new vista of possibilities and will reflect back to you some hidden potential in your character. This will contrast with what you've been experiencing in your existing or past relationships.

On the 10th, a lunar eclipse takes place in your domestic sphere and this brings with it a whole raft of emotional issues that will be hard to avoid until the 17th, at which point some breakthroughs can be expected—positive, I might add.

Tremendous opportunities for travel and getting about generally are on the cards from the 19th until the new Moon of the 25th. Spend this time ferreting out new opportunities, whether work or personal in nature. This month is a challenge but one which gives you some unforeseen opportunities if you maintain a vigilant awareness of the possibilities that come your way unasked for

Romance and friendship

If you spend too much time yapping on the phone on the 6th you'll find that your deadlines will eventually catch up with you and you'll have nothing to show for it. Balance your social and domestic obligations a little more carefully during this time frame.

On the 7th, if you tell a tall tale to win the approval of someone, it will damage your reputation when they learn the

TAURUS

brutal down-to-earth truth. State the facts, keeping the conversation black and white, and don't rely on dodgy information to embellish your story.

Your partner will be feeling more energetic and dynamic than usual, which will free up your time. Give them their own freedom on the 15th. This offers you the added bonus of cleaning up loose ends and spending quality time alone so you can get back in touch with those parts of your life that have been absent.

Around the 20th a dream can turn into a nightmare, especially where love is concerned. An idealistic partner is hard to find so don't for a minute think that a casual or one-night encounter is the end of your search. Keep your microscope with you and look as closely as possible at any character flaws you see.

You may have made peace with someone after a battle but will still have a sour taste in your mouth on the 16th. True forgiveness means moving forward with a clean slate even if you can't forget the incident completely. This is hard but essential to your happiness and things seem better after the 25th.

On the 26th, restless sleep is a sign that you aren't quite looking after yourself on either a mental or physical level. Take the right steps to ensure you get quality rest as well as sufficient time-out from stressful activities.

Work and money

You're highly strung and scattered for a day or so around the 8th. Don't go making plans on a whim, or worse still, committing yourself to something you haven't carefully thought through. This is where problems start. Use your energy to push through a creative concept that's been on the back burner for a while.

A gamble is ill-advised, especially on the 11th, if you're taking a tip from a casual gambler who hasn't got it straight

2009: FEBRUARY

themselves. You're better off considering slower and steadier returns on your money even if the investment doesn't pay as handsomely.

You have a greater determination between the 22nd and the 24th and should put that to good use. Achieving even more difficult goals will be easier under these transits. Your health is strong but don't push yourself beyond the limits of your physicality. Listen to what your body is saying to you.

You'll be worried about work and something that was said on the 28th. If you heard it on the grapevine, it's probably malicious gossip and will be irrelevant. If, on the other hand, a manager or someone in authority whispers in your ear, make some quick changes to get ahead of the rest.

Destiny dates

Positive: 3, 9, 10, 15, 17, 19, 21, 22, 23, 24, 25

Negative: 6, 7, 8, 11, 26, 28

Mixed: 20

MARCH

Highlights of the month

When the Moon is sitting near your Sun sign, and particularly after the 2nd, you're likely to be more emotional than you'd care to be. Many of your decisions will be based upon how you feel rather than how you think. Some of your assessments of others will also stem from past experiences that may not even be related to the person themselves.

I should give you a special tip, Taurus, which is that projecting your fears or bias on newcomers to your scene may adversely affect not only your peace of mind but opportunities that life will bring you. Around the 5th you should endeavour to be clear and concise in your communication and don't push topics into areas that you know are off-limits by others' standards.

The conjunction of Mars and Neptune is a very important one and can create a sense of ineffectual frustration with bosses and other co-workers who have the upper hand. You may know what needs to be done but will find yourself hamstrung and totally at odds with yourself and others.

This is a time of breathing deeply, taking up your yoga postures, or going for a run if you prefer. Anything rather than confrontation is suggested here as nothing else will probably

2009: MARCH

work, anyway. This is one of those occasions where you'll just have to grin and bear the situation.

A whole new sequence of possibilities emerges on the horizon from the 15th when Mars positively activates your zone of friendship and personal fulfilment. With the Sun also moving through this sector, it is unlikely you'll be left out of invitations to parties and other gatherings with some of them being work orientated. Don't miss out on what should be a heck of a lot of fun.

During this phase some further twists and turns can be anticipated through the interaction of the Sun and Uranus. If in the earlier months of the year you've found it hard to choose between conservative or progressive groups of friends, the decision will be very easy if not made for you by Providence itself.

Yes, 'different' will definitely appear better! An extraordinary introduction or connection will be made with some very unusual and off-beat individuals. This will excite you but is likely to also unnerve you, being conservative and not at all prone to change, as you are aware.

The new Moon on the 26th is a time when you can revisit such ideas as selfless service, community work and charitable activities to orientate your empathy towards a greater cause. The month finishes on a spiritual note.

Romance and friendship

Don't let family members rile you on the 4th. You're likely to give hair-trigger responses and this will ruin your day if you don't exercise emotional control. On a more positive note, someone on the home front does have a suggestion or two that can help move your career forward.

Try stepping out of your past self-image on the 9th. Progress means discarding anything useless. Sometimes that

TAURUS

means character traits and fashion icons to which we have become attached. No need for fear. Just experiment and see. If it doesn't work for you, revert back to your old ways without any stress.

If there is an assumption about you on the 17th, it will be wrong and this will have you reacting to set the record straight. This in turn will make you seem guiltier of something you're not. Either have an ally handy to back you up, or shut up and stop defending what's not true. The truth will come out on the 18th.

There's no way anyone will hold you back on the 23rd. You need to be out and about, exploring what life has on offer. If your gut feelings point you to a potential treasure trove—either romantically or socially—go full steam ahead. Your intuition will be right on track in your choice of friends, too.

If you can bridge the gap between your own and another's slightly different social opinions, it's quite likely that a raging romance is possible between you on the 27th. You need to let go of your initial concepts to fully appreciate this person's true personality.

If you are forceful in your opinions on the 29th you'll get what you want. But, don't necessarily think that it will endear you to those who think you're being a little too tough and self-centred. Your victory may have its downside as well.

Work and money

As quick as you'll be off the mark on the 5th, make sure that you have the correct facts on which to base your work. You might be fed incorrect details that will steer you in the wrong direction. Get clarity at the outset.

Starting a home business or working more comfortably from your residential premises is an added bonus if you can wangle it between the 7th and 11th. Additional investments are likely to be satisfying, with good returns.

2009: MARCH

Be open to others in your workplace as a new friendship is likely to commence and blossom on the 15th. By taking the time to listen to others' problems you will make them more relaxed in trusting you, and vice versa.

Success is attained through persistence between the 20th and the 25th. Don't say 'no' under any circumstances. It's the people that keep on keeping on that end up being victorious. You'll come out the victor if you keep your eye on the ball.

Destiny dates

Positive: 7, 8, 9, 10, 11, 15, 18, 20, 21, 22, 23, 24, 25, 26, 27

Negative: 2, 4, 5

Mixed: 5, 17, 29

APRIL

Highlights of the month

When Mars and Saturn move into difficult aspects, as they will in the first week of April, the going can get pretty tough. Frustrations and also continuing unfulfilled desires may plague you. In some cases a member of the family may be unable to be helped and this can be the source of tremendous anxiety.

For your information, Saturn is a very friendly planet to your ruling planet Venus, and this is a mystical secret that you should use to overcome this temporary difficulty. The secret is this: Saturn being a planet of discipline opposes the impulsive and rash behaviour of Mars, its enemy. This simply means to resist the tendency to shoot from the hip, to aggressively grab control of someone's feelings or their circumstances.

Between the 5th and 10th, children may feature in this equation and the advice I am giving you is this: Do not under any circumstances try to grapple or coerce someone into changing their position. Restrain yourself and utilise the friendly energies of Saturn to help this person through their difficult times.

Simply listening is enough. You don't have to push them in any direction, just let their own wisdom come to them in their own good time. You'll maintain a good relationship with them and, after the 15th when the Moon does its thing with Pluto, you may finally get to the bottom of the issue, remove it permanently from your life and feel transformed in the process.

Love affairs prosper between the 12th and 15th, but after this you should avoid risky adventures romantically, particularly with people you don't know all that well. You will exaggerate the virtues or talents of someone and could kick yourself afterwards when you learn the truth. Venture into all new relationships with your eyes wide open and lips sealed tight. Observe before you act.

Both Venus and Mars enter your zone of secrets on the 22nd and the 23rd of April. There is something mysterious yet passionate about this combination and, to be honest with you, I smell a rat! There may be something underhanded and deceptive about relationships at this time and, God forbid, even your hand in the deception.

Keep all your relationships above board and if you do so you'll feel renewed by the 25th of the new Moon, which happens to be again in your Sun sign of Taurus.

Financial matters and contracts could be in the spotlight between the 26th and 28th when some good fortune takes place with your demands being met promptly.

Romance and friendship

Communication with your spouse or partner is much better on the 5th. You're able to express how you feel and vice versa. There is also the likelihood of humour playing a more important role in cementing friendships. You don't need to be too serious to make headway in love.

You'll find that getting angry doesn't win you any Brownie points and will therefore be useless in trying to change things. On the 9th or 10th, if others are annoying you, are not

TAURUS

performing to your highest standards or responding correctly, then blasting them will only create more trouble. Try a new tactic.

If your partner is being lazy and unmotivated on the 8th, don't worry because things are about to change for the better. You'll see a greater effort to support you and participate in your activities, especially after the 15th. A fun and sociable attitude also helps decompress any tensions you might have been experiencing in love.

That feeling of not being loved or appreciated will bother you between the 20th and the 22nd. All things are subject to cycles in nature and love is no different. You will feel warmer in your affection and so will your partner, as long as you don't let this feeling snowball. It's important not to hold grudges or carry around past hurts that can't be changed. Accept your situation calmly.

Love may be on the back burner for a while from the 23rd, but it doesn't mean completely ignoring your responsibilities to the person you love most in your life. It doesn't have to be an all-or-nothing type of period. Moderation and compromise will result in a win–win situation on the new Moon of the 25th. The last week of the month should give your romantic life a distinct lift.

Work and money

Your urge to take a gamble should be curbed as winning the big one may not be destined for you on the 5th. Thinking about the consequences is essential to spare you regrets in the future. The difficulty is in the company you keep. Be careful.

Your mind is so quick and accurate on the 12th that you'll surprise yourself when you see through the mind games of a work colleague or friend. Your detective-like vigilance will help uncover a part of someone's character that wasn't previously obvious. It's time for a peer group shake up!

2009: APRIL

Be the deal broker on the 18th! Creatively bringing several parties together on a deal is the way you can successfully solve a financial dilemma. There is definitely strength in numbers and you'll be surprised to learn that the other people are thinking along similar lines to you.

On the 24th, something you misplaced may mysteriously re-appear, much to your surprise and satisfaction. If you like to tuck things away safely and make sure you don't forget where you've hidden them, in this case you might have concealed the item too well. Anyhow, you breathe a sigh of relief.

Destiny dates

Positive: 12, 13, 14, 15, 18, 24, 25, 26, 27, 28

Negative: 9, 10, 20, 21, 22, 23

Mixed: 5, 6, 7, 8, 9, 10, 23

MAY

Highlights of the month

Many happy returns, Taurus; it's during this period of the year that the Sun makes its return to Taurus thereby endowing you with a bright and attractive energy. This will make you extremely popular and, who knows, possibly capable of conquering the world!

For some attached Taureans, choosing between your partner and other external 'distractions' may cause some fights or at least tense moments this month. A reconciliatory position can be reached by the 5th as Mercury will perfect your speech and cause others to be more amenable to your position. Try to avoid misunderstandings if you can.

An undercurrent of clandestine energy continues from last month, and mustn't steer you in the wrong direction. You must use your solar powers for a good rather than a negative outcome. You'll attract all sorts of people into your orb this month and by the 9th this will be obvious. Making choices between friends or groups of people perhaps may weigh heavily upon you.

Mercury also brings with it a certain amount of cleverness, particularly in the area of your finances. This is not only a practical and resourceful transit but you may come up with some

2009: MAY

brilliant new ideas that will not initially seem commercially viable. But they will be in time!

Negotiating a good deal for yourself after the 15th can pay off handsomely by the 17th or 18th. If the deal isn't brokered immediately don't become disheartened. Persist and success will be yours when you least expect it.

A relative or close friend may suffer some health problems this month. You'll be required to make the effort and, even if this is hard and the problem is not particularly serious, you'll know that it will be almost impossible to sidestep the issue as you may lose face in the process.

Excellent financial opportunities again occur on the 24th and a new scheme or possibly even a business or work opportunity will arise out of nowhere. You can take this opportunity and prepare for a new phase in your working life. A reunion on the home front in the last few days of the month will warm your heart.

Romance and friendship

A new love affair can be distracting on the 3rd. You will be unable to concentrate on anything other than the person. The reverse may be true as well if there is a problem that is haunting you. The thought will be going round and round your brain like a cracked record. Break the spell and think of other worthwhile matters.

Your view of a situation will become crystal clear on the 6th. Confusion is lifting with the result that you know what has to be done. That will also be difficult because the situation will leave you in no doubt as to the appropriate course of action. Are you brave enough to act now?

Harness as much energy as you can between the 9th and the 16th you're going to need it. You will be tempted to believe falsely that you have an endless supply of time and

TAURUS

resources for others. Apply the global warming attitude to your own personal energy supplies; that is, conservation!

Someone's advice skews. If you make a decision based upon their 'reliable' information you will be quite peeved off at this fact. The only thing you can do on the 18th is make the best of the situation and exercise more caution in future.

Don't demand more time of a friend than they can afford right on the 26th. You might come across as selfish and scare them off. It's more a case of quality versus quantity but in the heat of the moment you may overlook this fact. Be thankful for small graces.

Your focus on the 28th seems to be on your health. Take the time to listen to your body signals and don't ignore those early vital signs. Trust your bodily intuition.

Work and money

You're in your element with the Sun moving through your own sign this month. It means that your business instincts are coming to the fore and your mental attitude is strong. You can afford to push the envelope a little on the 7th and score a 'goal' financially.

On the 9th, just as you thought you had a deal or project in the bag, some idiot will want to dredge up irrelevant details and slow the process to a grinding halt. If they have the upper hand you'll have to agree, grin and bear it. On the other hand, if *you* have the power you can have a lot of fun kicking them into the kerb.

There are either choices at work, or choices *between* different jobs on the 15th. Decisions, decisions! I think this is more to do with a choice within yourself; that is, how you want to live your life rather than what job you think is IT. Self-examination is the key.

Property matters are disturbing, especially if you overspend on the 29th! Take it easy; you don't have to have everything the Jones's have, right? Try to be a little more content with the simple things in life and the bigger stuff will arrive on its own.

Destiny dates

Positive: 5, 6, 7, 10, 11, 12, 13, 14, 15, 16, 17, 24

Negative: 29

Mixed: 3, 9, 15, 18, 26, 28

Highlights of the month

If I had the opportunity to take some of your friends and colleagues to the side, I'd whisper a few quiet words in their ear this month and tell them to step out of your way. Without any doubt Mars will pump you up and have you stomping on anyone that gets in your path. You mean business and your competitive urges will be very outstanding.

Between the 1st and the 8th your outwardly directed concerns will mean that you bring your demands to the table and won't cop any flack from anyone. You'll be more animated and aggressive than people expect you to be and this might just create an avalanche of negative repercussions if you're not careful.

You'll probably have some self-doubts, which will cause you to overcompensate, so make sure your reason for going head to head with others is at least based on the right motives. Sure, you'll get what you want, but at what cost?

It's best to redirect your drive and ambitious exploits to your work and moneymaking enterprises rather than family. You can achieve a lot, especially after the 13th and then again between the 20th and 23rd. The planets will augment and help redirect and lift your vibrant energy into constructive channels.

2009: JUNE

The key issues this month centre around having a clear understanding of who you are and where you'd like to be in the larger scheme of life. People will see through any charade that rests on a lack of confidence or insufficient facts or information. There's no way you'll be able to improvise your way through important meetings or even social encounters. Don't let your cockiness over-inflate your ego after the 22nd as you may find yourself in an embarrassing predicament that will take extra time to rectify.

One safe haven will be your home with fortune apparently resting in the most obvious place of all, your backyard. I don't just mean material fortune but peace of mind and general satisfaction. In the last week of June, why not put some long overdue energy into your family relationships, and in particular, your mother, father and their relations. This will defuse some of the Martian explosions before they cause too much damage.

Watch your health in the last couple of days of the month, making sure not to skip meals nor eat food that is not in keeping with your body type. You'll feel the signals pretty quickly.

Romance and friendship

The universe will throw you a curved ball in the relationships department on the 4th. A friend will demand more of you. This will tantalise you even if you know in your heart you shouldn't go there.

On the 11th a goodbye needn't be a sad affair. Concentrate on what you've learned, the fun times you've had and the fine memories you will take into the future. The story with someone is over, so accept it. You'll feel much freer.

You'll see the serious side of someone threatening the stability of your group between the 13th and 17th but will fully

TAURUS

sympathise with their rather severe or stern attitude, having been there and done that yourself. It's an opportunity to take them aside and let them know how it feels.

You can become younger yourself by associating with younger people on the 19th. Don't turn away from an exceptional opportunity that will be offered by one of your kids if you're a parent. Younger co-workers also have a surprise for you.

You've outgrown some of your religious viewpoints as a life necessity, so why would you feel guilty? Are you carrying superimposed ethics around in your back pocket? Not good. Get rid of what is non-essential on the 9th and don't let friends make you feel guilty about your beliefs.

On the 23rd, wait for some free time to make that long-distance phone call (unless you have an Internet connection that isn't costly). You might get carried away by the moment and forget that your phone bill will ultimately arrive. Oh well, it will be fun while it lasts!

You may find yourself at odds with social or cultural standards on the 30th. But that's okay, because love and beauty is in the eye of the beholder, so fully allow yourself to trust your feelings and discard any preconceived ideas of what the perfect lover should be like.

Work and money

Thinking big has its upside and downside on the 12th. You're way ahead of the pack, but if and when someone asks the legitimate question of where you'll get the resources for conquering the world, don't get defensive. It's a fair question.

Your work will be fulfilling on the 14th, so enjoy it if you can. Careful scrutiny is necessary to drive home your point to a disbeliever or sceptic. Let the facts speak for themselves once your research is done.

2009: JUNE

Spend money beautifying your surroundings, whether at work or at home on the 22nd; it will do you the world of good. Pay attention to colours as these will also enhance your sense of wellbeing. Make shopping a social occasion at the same time.

Allow yourself the luxury of a little lethargy—even a quiet sleep—if your body tells you this is the way to go on the 28th. You need some relief during this particularly busy cycle. By doing so you'll knock the edge off that irritable side to your nature at this time, too.

Destiny dates

Positive: 13, 14, 19, 20, 21, 23, 28

Negative: Nil

Mixed: 1, 2, 3, 4, 5, 6, 7, 8, 11, 12, 13, 14, 15, 16, 17, 22

JULY

Highlights of the month

Your search and drive for independence reaches a peak at this time of the year with progressive Uranus gaining momentum in its reverse motion. You are still bothered by the forces that are shaping intimate friendships and need to continue working on your relationships with certain key individuals.

Believe it or not, the full Moon and lunar eclipse on the 7th point to unresolved issues stemming from your parental interactions as a child and could now be impacting upon your social experiences. Before pointing the finger at anyone, look carefully at what it is you're doing that is destabilising these parts of your life.

Up until the 11th there will be a mixture of financial and personal responsibilities overshadowing your sense of wellbeing. This will act as a background against the continuing combination of passionate Mars and Venus. You'll be torn in many different directions and I feel that after the 12th some arguments over money could further cloud the issues that are really at the heart of any problem you'll be dealing with.

Home really is where the heart is and around the 18th Mercury brings to a conclusion many negotiations with a positive outcome for all involved. Until the 25th you may shy away from work and professional pressures in favour of improving relations on the home front.

Around the new Moon of the 22nd until the 28th, friendships in your neighbourhood or an improvement of your connection with a sibling will make you feel that July has not been a complete waste of time.

In the last two days of the month, please don't exaggerate your statements or employ second-hand facts and information to argue a point. The people you'll be dealing with are probably a step ahead of you and this will undermine your reputation, your credibility and self-respect. You can, however, use analogies and tell a few comical stories that will secure a deal or negotiation, especially if you happen to be involved in sales, marketing or advertising.

The important combination for you this month is the Venus–Mars relationship, which, for married Taureans is significant and, although challenging, can give a wonderful result in cementing love and goodwill. Don't give up even if the going gets tough.

Romance and friendship

Relationships never end, they just keep growing! Even though the form of the relationship certainly changes, you don't need to throw the baby out with the bath water on the 4th. Try to see the deeper side of your karmic connections and, once certain lessons have been learned, the association will then assume a different shape, if only just friendship. Stop trying to pigeonhole your friendships.

Simply refuse to play mind games on the 13th and 14th when someone throws down the gauntlet. Once you begin to play by their rules, you've lost. It's simply a matter of sticking to your guns and letting others understand clearly that you're not going to play psychological warfare with them.

TAURUS

On the 16th, the Mars and Neptune aspect makes you vulnerable to certain allergies, foods and even medicinal compounds. Trust your body signals in this matter and, if you feel the least trace of a reaction, particularly regarding a food or substance you've never tried before, discontinue its use.

It's advisable to think twice about a possible trip or change of lifestyle on the 22nd. Settling back into your tried and tested way of life is the way to go. You're probably feeling more appreciative of the circumstances you're in as well. Being less impulsive offers more security now.

You're in two minds about love, sex and marriage from the 28th until the 31st. You've lost interest in the traditional approach and think the whole romance game is overrated. This still doesn't solve the problem of your desires, though—through which you need love and affection and a creative outlet for your instincts. You'll work it out but only if you're absolutely honest with your feelings.

Work and money

Work takes precedence between the 8th and the 12th, but you're probably over-emphasising the amount of energy you need to put into your task because it's turning out to be a case of needing a sledgehammer to crack open a walnut. Just unwind, sit back and identify what needs to be done and then let nature take its course. Don't give yourself any heartache when it's not necessary.

You feel an obligation to enhance yourself on the 9th. You can't force yourself into an area before it's time. Soon enough you'll feel more confident about pursuing a new line of study or direction in life. Till then don't allow a feeling of obligation to dominate you.

You're hardly likely to want to change a decision or intellectual position you've taken on the 16th, but flexibility will be seen by others as a mark of your graciousness. If you maintain a stubborn position on the issue you will do more harm than good. Be seen to be open and receptive to others' opinions.

Get all your paperwork together on the 23rd and don't be afraid to look at the truth of your net worth. Once you see things as they are, your mind will be clearer and you'll be in a better position to know just how much you have and exactly when to spend your money.

Destiny dates

Positive: 18, 19, 20, 21, 22, 23, 24, 25, 26, 27, 28

Negative: 9, 12, 13, 14

Mixed: 4, 7, 8, 9, 10, 11, 12, 16, 22, 28, 29, 30, 31

AUGUST

Highlights of the month

The full Moon of August can bring considerable new insights about your work, so don't be too alarmed by the changes that are happening. For the most part this is a time where your attention to detail and your awareness of industry changes can help you forge ahead with new techniques and methodologies and this is all positive stuff for you.

Over and above your work, let your hair down, kick your heels up and get ready to party this month, Taurus. Venus enters your zone of communications, short journeys and song and dance on the 1st. You'll be more outgoing, less concerned by long-term troubles and your stress factor will drop thus giving you a feeling of wellbeing.

Between the 2nd and 10th Venus and Pluto produce some intense feelings and you won't be able to help express how you're feeling about someone at this time. During the same phase Mercury, the sprightly, communicative planet, triggers your romance and creative zone and this is further testimony to an intense relationship with which you will be preoccupied.

On occasions I see this combination result in obsessive qualities and it may be stemming from yourself, or another person who is the object of your affection. If you're entering a new relationship it's not a bad idea to create some boundaries at the outset to avoid later misunderstandings.

There's a strong Scorpio quality about this match and the person in question. You may find that issues of possessiveness and inflexibility are somewhat limiting to your or their independence. There's no use beating around the bush and pretending everything is okay, particularly around the lunar eclipse of the 6th when it's important for you to express your feelings and clear the air.

You could be nervous, highly strung and a little out of whack around the 22nd, so plan carefully rather than acting on the spur of the moment. Your nerves are likely to be blown apart by taking on far too many projects simply for the sake of pleasing others or maybe for just looking cool. Trust your intuition and say no if you feel you can't deliver.

Up to the 26th there's no doubt you'll have ample opportunity to mix with bright, energetic and mentally stimulating people. Physically you will also be strong. Mars moves into a powerful position around the 26th giving you not only physical prowess but mental stamina and determination of will.

This is not a time for anyone to stand in your way or refuse your ideas. You could, in a huff, walk out on a situation, possibly even your job, on the 27th if you meet any resistance to the plans you've set in place.

Remain calm between the 28th and the 31st because you're likely to magnify a comment out of all proportion. Try to see the bright side of things and don't act impulsively until this phase passes.

Romance and friendship

You need a far greater overview of your relationships on the 8th. A mishmash of psychological, philosophical and even sexual issues will create cross-signals with those whom you're

TAURUS

trying get on. Unless you know what you want there's no point trying to superimpose your desires by making demands on others. I suspect you sense this is the case, and will need to own up to it.

The pleasure loving side of your nature would prefer to opt for the ease of social interaction rather than follow your instinctive sense of practicality on the 10th. At home things will be in disarray up until the 16th and need your immediate attention. How will you possibly enjoy a night out on the town with these problems gnawing away at your heartstrings? First things first.

Exotic houses, buildings and other flamboyant architectural wonders may inspire you to pay more attention to your residence and somehow get something of similar grandeur on the 20th.

On the 23rd tell your partner that hoarding your pennies shouldn't be seen as anything other than your desire to share a good life together. You should balance your visionary exploits with the needs of those you love and with whom you'll ultimately share these acquisitions.

You can't use ultimatums to gain your ends in your family circle on the 27th. These strategies just don't work and, what's more, if you happen to be indebted to a relative with whom you don't particularly get along, these strategies will not only create upset but breed resentment. Try alternative methods of communicating to get what you want.

You can make a breakthrough in your relationship on the 30th. It's as if you'll connect so much more easily with someone. This could be the start of even better things.

Work and money

You mustn't take your daily routine too much for granted as everything around will be changing on the 3rd. Using the same

2009: AUGUST

old timetables that worked before may not do so on the 5th. By becoming stuck in a way of doing things, your schedule can fall apart.

On the 6th you have to make some time to reorganise your habits and reinvent itineraries. You will look to experts or others whom you feel are more capable of doing this, but ultimately this is a do-it-yourself issue.

Even if you want to push through financial or business negotiations it will result in a setback if not a disappointment from the 16th to the 21st. You must be on guard not to mix commercial interests with friendships or rely too much on the referrals of others. Make your own decisions and take more time to do so.

Stop hiding behind your desk; you've got to make important communications if you're trying to network yourself and gain a strategic advantage. Make appropriate adjustments on the 23rd both in terms of your time and the activity and people with whom you're dealing. Ignoring others and finding excuses for not returning calls is in no way useful to your objectives.

Destiny dates

Positive: 6, 23, 26, 30

Negative: 5, 16, 17, 18, 19, 21, 22, 23, 27

Mixed: 2, 3, 4, 5, 6, 7, 8, 9, 10, 20, 27, 28, 29, 30, 31

SEPTEMBER

Highlights of the month

Brace yourself for a month of increasing responsibility. Now, I must point out that, although I say your duties and responsibilities could be heavier throughout September, it doesn't mean you can't still enjoy the pressure, the respect and honour that come with acquiring a better position in life.

Around the 7th there could be a conflict between how you want to present yourself and what is expected of you. Try to be clear about whether your ego is getting in the way of your success. You may have to eat humble pie for a few days to secure your position in a new role.

Mercury moves into retrogression in your zone of work and daily routine. Continue to adjust yourself, even if it seems hard at first. Ample rewards will be yours as a result.

Working on health and dietary issues will also be important to you this month. By the 19th you'll have in place a whole new schedule that will encompass your daily exercise, diet and possibly an alteration to the way you conduct appointments and meetings to make the best use of your time. Efficiency will be high on your agenda.

You'll be looking at new ways of doing things and you'll have to lift your ball game to break the habit of falling back on old techniques and systems that are outmoded. Gadgetry and other computing devices that can enhance your output and make life easier for you will not be easy to get your head around.

But, you must try, because this is what will set the trend for the next few months, offering you even greater successes. Between the 16th and 23rd you'll be called upon to dig deep and come up with some brilliant and creative new solutions. Kill two birds with one stone, I say, because some of the problems you may encounter with children or young people can be solved using the same strategies as you'll need to employ in your professional arena.

Serious and deliberate thinking will win the day after the 24th. The focus is on metaphysical ideas and how your thinking affects your destiny. Don't be rushed into decisions as Mercury and Saturn conjoin to bring you better outcomes through deliberation. You'll feel comfortable in this mode of thought and mustn't let others convince you otherwise.

This is a month where you have to rethink some of your plans and goals, so when Mercury moves into its direct motion on the 29th, you'll feel tremendously relieved at the prospect of being able to practically put in place some of your ideas.

Strong family bonds should cause you to anticipate reunions and some sort of important family get-together that has a very nostalgic feel to it. Someone from your family's past may re-emerge and rekindle many old memories.

Romance and friendship

Projecting your disappointment and expectations on friends is really a recipe for disaster if you're trying to establish a better connection and more quality relationships on the 3rd. The people you're pointing the finger at are the ones who may be most able to help you get out of the rut you're in.

TAURUS

Make a list of those activities that seem to be emotionally satisfying to you on the full Moon of the 4th and this will help you find the path of least resistance in which you can feel passionate about what you do *with* those whom you want to spend your time.

You may be over-sensitive by feeling that someone isn't making as much effort as you are on the 8th. You will feel as if they are not as committed to the friendship. There are different ways of expressing how you feel and you may be overlooking some of their more subtle and important contributions to the relationship. Look more attentively to what they have contributed in the past. You'll see the other side of the story.

Between the 12th and the 18th you will want impromptu outings but will find yourself out of your depth when the company you happen to fall in with becomes a bit strange. Although you are not totally adverse to trying new things and meeting new people, this cycle will be just a little too strange, even for your tastes. It's not a bad idea to get a preview from friends as to who may be a part of the action.

You may be hurt by aggressive or dominating people between the 22nd and the 25th. If you are confronted by this kind of person, you will react in an emotional manner. Your response will irritate them and they will resent you for it. You have to make a show of strength, though.

Work and money

Finances need a little more tweaking on the 10th and the 11th as some of the overheads that you take for granted as being outside your normal field of vision are significant enough to worry about. These small ongoing costs add up and, unless you're committed to cutting back in these areas, you won't make significant inroads as far as savings and future security are concerned. It's a mini-cycle of saving rather than spending.

2009: SEPTEMBER

Upholding your credit rating is important on the 19th but debts will tend to outstrip your earnings with the result that not only do your financial objectives slow down to a snail's pace but your mind may be worried. There's a simple way to stop debt dead in its tracks: don't spend money.

Have you thought of re-establishing old work contacts from your past? The period of the 28th to the 30th is strong to draw you back into the past and utilise the expertise of those people who were formative or significant in terms of your professional life. By travelling and spending time in such places, deeper, unresolved issues can come to the surface and be cleared for spiritual growth.

Destiny dates

Positive: 4, 16, 17, 18, 20, 21, 28, 29, 30

Negative: 7, 3, 25

Mixed: 10, 11, 12, 13, 14, 15, 16, 17, 18, 19, 22, 23, 24

OCTOBER

Highlights of the month

If you have planned your finances well, you should find some surplus cash this month with which to enjoy life. There are indeed some natives of Taurus who'd like to live for the moment, being drawn to the sensate pleasures and, if you tend to lean towards that, this month may prove to you that spending on the spur of the moment does have some undesirable side-effects; namely, debt.

Get some advice on how to manage your money if you're feeling confused. Even if you are less of a spendthrift and manage your money well, it's not a bad idea to take some good advice or hang out with friends in the know. It's amazing what you'll pick up and you needn't apply their suggestions without first testing the water, but you'll certainly learn something new about how to better manage your money and get a greater return on your investments.

Jupiter is powerful after the 13th October and, for Taureans who have been waiting for the green light on a new position or better lifestyle, you will be pleased that this could be the turning point you've been waiting for. There may be some compromises to be made, however, because Venus and Saturn moving in the zone of love affairs make it hard for you to feel totally fulfilled in both professional and personal areas of your life simultaneously.

You need to work hard to explain to your friends and family that, for a while, you may not be as available as you'd like to be. You can see this as a grand opportunity and so will not be too concerned about any sacrifice that has to be made.

Helping others to achieve their success will be an important component of your life throughout the last three months of 2009. The law of the universe which suggests that helping others will also indirectly help you, will become more of a tangible experience rather than theory at this time.

From the 15th to the 20th you'll render good service to others by forfeiting any thought of personal benefit. If you've been investigating the possibilities of spiritual evolution and karmic development you will experience a whole new state of mind, which will be simply offering your expertise without any thought for gain. This will win you some new friends and allies.

A complication with a family member's finances needn't embroil you in a battle if you're diplomatic about the advice you give and where you stand between the two parties around the 24th. As long as you're asking questions, you can't put a foot wrong. Hold back before offering your views. October comes to an interesting conclusion with Saturn moving towards the zone of work and efficiency and heralds the commencement of a new two-and-a-half-year cycle in your workplace.

Romance and friendship

You won't get the response you desire on the 4th but at least your peers will know exactly where you stand and that you're not afraid to be brutally honest when the occasion warrants it.

Dealing with the emotions of a family member will either cause you to fall apart or offer you an alternative opportunity

TAURUS

to test your own metal and handle things on the 12th. If you get sucked into the serve–volley emotional tennis match that arises out of the bad behaviour of others, you'll find yourself no better than your competitor. Don't be offended by what is simply someone's personal problem.

You will have to help someone to express their secret feelings on the 18th. But people don't always believe you are genuinely interested in them. Be careful because by trying to extract too much information too soon, you will be regarded as a busybody. Control your curiosity and let someone lead you instead.

Your best response on the 24th will be silence as it will be almost impossible for anyone to pigeonhole an opinion that is elusive. Leaving a co-worker or friend second-guessing is far superior to being misinterpreted, don't you agree? Use your words sparingly as this will be your greatest weapon under these planetary transits. Mars will be inciting you to war, so resist!

Acceleration seems to be the key word on the 29th but the world will seem to be moving in slow motion compared with you. Have you considered that moving others at an exponential rate to catch up with you will not be possible and that travelling to your destination will have to be done alone at times? Someone's reluctance to take your lead, and pushing them to an unnatural pace, will only create resistance.

Work and money

You will look at a conservative plan to improve your finances around the 7th. Don't fall victim to the high-yield dangling carrot when your gut feeling tells you to move more slowly. The smooth-talking sales person will want a piece of your bank balance, so watch out.

Your karmic planets bring you in touch with abrasive elements in your working environment between the 17th and the 25th; but, interestingly, you will be attracted to someone

2009: OCTOBER

who acts as a timely ally against common foes! You will realise that not all relationships are for keeps but coming together for a common good at this time will serve both of you, if only temporarily.

If for some reason you don't feel all that creative professionally on the 26th, there are other ways in which you can express your giftedness. Do what you can at work but find other outlets to compensate for the time being. Cooking, decorating your home and doing other handy crafts are ways for you to escape the humdrum routine of day-to-day life and feel spiritually uplifted. Your creativity returns to a high point on the 29th, but you must determine how best to direct those energies.

Destiny dates

Positive: 13, 15, 16, 17, 18, 19, 20, 21, 22, 23, 24, 25, 26

Negative: 7

Mixed: 12, 18, 24, 29

NOVEMBER

Highlights of the month

You may be challenged to try something different this month, to go to places you've never been before and mix with people whom you would previously have avoided. You will feel an inward push to step outside your normal way of seeing things and this is one of the luckiest types of energy that you will be blessed with, as it will steer you into many new opportunities and friendships. Have no fear.

You have psychic antennae this month and, if your creative and communicative power isn't enough, having these premonitions is going to put you a step ahead of others. You can see other people's thoughts and anticipate what they're going to say, which means your business skills will be enhanced. Between the 5th and 7th, seize an opportunity that is presented, even if it doesn't seem to have much profit or benefit at the outset. This could be the proverbial iceberg of which you're only seeing the tip.

As Venus moves into the zone of marriage on the 8th, your romantic feelings are idealised and some Taureans may even be ready to tie the knot. Love, warmth and reciprocal affection can be expected at this time. Actually, I might add that Venus's presence in this part of the zodiac could make you a little too attractive thereby attracting more than one potential lover! You'll need to come up with some good excuses as to why you don't want to pursue a friendship. I guess the other alternative would be to learn the art of juggling.

I mentioned that this period of the year could see you acquiring some new role, an opportunity in which your power and authority is enhanced, but would you be surprised if I told you there may also be some secret enemies lurking in the shadows? People who might try with great effort to undermine this authority? Be prepared to justify your actions and your course of action generally when you meet with opposition.

Of course, there may be no rhyme or reason other than envy and the tall poppy syndrome; but, as mentioned in the previous months, let your diplomacy deal with these people. Don't buy into squabbles and ego trips or mind games. You'll come out a winner after the 22nd looking all that much better to your peers for keeping your cool and not playing these games on the terms of others.

You are also likely to take interest in the market forces shaping the value of property and land. It is a good time to look at that if you're considering it as a form of investment, because it suits your Taurus nature perfectly; being an earth sign like the land. This has much to do with dynamic Mars passing through your property and real estate zone during this second last month of the year.

There may be some minor health problems that will be quickly alleviated if there is prompt action on your part. Lower back problems should be attended to immediately so as not to cause further distress to you. There is also the opportunity of meeting someone in the health or healing arts who will fascinate you and become a friend.

TAURUS

Romance and friendship

You have a sneaking suspicion about someone's character on the 2nd but find yourself between a rock and a hard place in sharing this information with anyone else. It's one of those instances in which cold hard facts are not available and others probably wouldn't believe you, anyhow. This is your intuition working at its best and whatever it's telling you about someone needs to be heeded.

Connecting with important male figures of your past (most notably represented by your father) are key issues in your personal growth between the 14th and the 19th. The way you communicate or receive communication from men in authority will be a powerful reflection of your development. An important meeting around the 22nd will be a barometer of just how much you've learned.

Your moods can reach a new positive pinnacle on the 23rd because of Venus and Neptune. This can make you unusually prone to flights of imagination or simply daydreaming. Something on which you've hung your hat or expect to eventuate may end up offering you a perfectly strange twist to your life around the 25th. Although the stability of your life may be jeopardised, you won't care. It's a period of surprises but be prepared and under no circumstances rock the boat if it's not necessary.

Incorrectly judging people on the 27th will be a sure sign that you still haven't learnt some of your most valuable karmic lessons.

Venus and the Moon cast their favourable influence on you on the 29th, so you'll want to reward yourself. You'll appreciate yourself without any of the past emotional baggage or self-deprecation that rears its head from time to time. Share some romantic moments with a loved one. You will feel inspired by someone older than yourself who is quicker to see your good points than you are.

Work and money

You are stimulated by a whole bunch of new ideas and your imagination may even start to run a little wild with you on the 4th and 5th. Your drive is strong to achieve success. New business associations formed at this time will move to a profitable level quicker than you expect. There will be some good news on the income question.

Your working life is bound to be a source of great pleasure on the 13th and older people in the form of professional mentors are prepared to spend time with you. They will give you assistance in achieving some short-term goals.

Some of your ambitions and plans for success will take on a higher priority between the 16th and 22nd. Remain focused on those things that matter and discard anything that is distracting you from practical application. Exercise some of your down-to-earth qualities now to gain what you want.

You will be quite confused on the 25th. The planets accentuate your ego as well as your desire to help someone in a fix on the 28th. You'll be pulling yourself back into a somewhat self-absorbed state, though. Which will it be? You will try to be both, perhaps.

Destiny dates

Positive: 4, 5, 6, 7, 8, 13, 14, 15, 16, 17, 18, 19, 20, 21, 22, 23, 29

Negative: 2, 27, 25

Mixed: 25, 28

DECEMBER

Highlights of the month

At last, you'll find resolution in your social sphere in December. Just as well; you wouldn't want to have these sorts of confusing and mixed signals dampening your Christmas spirit, would you?

On the 2nd to the 6th you'll be able to get on with relationships and move forward in your life as a whole. There could be a large gift or some unexpected windfall at this time due to the Sun, Mercury and Venus occupying the hidden eighth zone of your horoscope. You're lucky this month and your big thinking underpins your magnet-like qualities.

You will attract good things due to the full Moon and new Moon influencing your income and shared financial resources. If you need a business partner or investor in an idea you should try this month to approach them with good response.

Educational pursuits you would think would be winding down at the close of the year will actually become stimulated after the 7th due to Mercury and Pluto arousing your curiosity. You're interested to know more about people, even those you've known for a long time. They could start to be a little concerned about your sudden interest in the mystery of their past, their interests and other deeper personality traits.

This has a strong psychological tone to it and also causes you to ask more introspective questions of yourself. This can only be good because such a starting point for improved relationships with everyone will result in a deeper understanding of your own character. I totally encourage this.

Just before Christmas, Mars, your relationship planet, moves into reverse gear and indicates your partner or spouse might have second thoughts about an agreement you thought was in the bag. Don't discuss it until after the festive season as you're likely to stir up a hornet's nest.

In the last days of the month, with Venus entering the journey zone of your horoscope, it's more than likely a pleasurable holiday, which is tied in with romance, is on the cards. Make sure you have all your travel arrangements settled before the 27th, at which point some born under Taurus might impulsively decide to get away. Not a good idea! If you haven't purchased your tickets, stay put and don't confuse the issue by making life harder for yourself.

After the 28th your mind will be in a quiet, carefree state with little worry for anyone else. I wouldn't be surprised to find you're feeling quite happy in your own skin, doing your own thing, without the hassle of others. One of the final planetary aspects for Taurus is the Venus-conjunction-with-Pluto scenario. That previous obsessive relationship I spoke to you about earlier in the year may now be ready to come to fruition.

Romance and friendship

Do you want to be the centre of attention or would you prefer to stay away from the hustle and bustle of social activity for just a little while? I would suggest you don't waste a great social opportunity to push forward as hard and fast as you can right on the 2nd. You can rest later in the month.

TAURUS

It is clear that you'll have to keep your wits about you in friendship between the 7th and the 13th. There will be warring factions and disputes that call for your help in mediating those problems (this seems to be a continuing theme right up to the end of the year). You'll become very involved in the discussions (heated ones at that) of those you are constantly in touch with on a day-to-day basis. This will be a real challenge for you but will make you feel good that you've helped out.

The Sun tugs at your spiritual heartstrings on the 16th and it will be steering you towards a quieter environment that you will find pretty hard to resist. You need some answers but no one on the outside is going to give them to you. This is an inner solution. The flashes of brilliance that come to you will be from your higher self or some spiritual guide and will be prominent between the 16th and 19th.

Your values will be challenged, so it's important to balance tradition with forward thinking. You'll be much clearer about what course of action you wish to take and it may be that you're ready to let go of some of the value systems that you carried earlier and are no longer useful.

Relationships will be a struggle around the 20th and 21st. This is due to you grappling with authority and conservative values. Trust your instincts and let love—that is, your heart and not your head—help you decide the proper course of action.

Work and money

Working with equilibrium creates a very calming effect on the 1st and 2nd. By remaining unruffled you can see others' motivations more clearly and will therefore respond with far greater efficiency and impact.

You're walking the line between conservatism and brilliant, original visions on the 7th. Tread carefully as someone may shoot you down in flames before you get the idea up and

2009: DECEMBER

running. Don't show your hand and wait until others are warm to your concepts.

If you're feeling stuck on the 11th it's only a matter of time before you see yourself free again. Things are moving slower and more deliberately, which in itself is not a bad thing. You'll have the opportunity to consider the facts a little more carefully than you normally would. Expect a move forward on the 19th.

You can imagine alternatives for your character and how you present yourself to the world but, until you practise what you visualise, you'll never know what the reaction from others will be. On the 23rd, step out of your normal routine and try some different looks to gain the attention you seek.

Destiny dates

Positive: 1, 2, 3, 4, 5, 6, 7, 19, 23, 27, 28

Negative: 11, 20, 21

Mixed: 7, 8, 9, 10, 11, 12, 13, 16

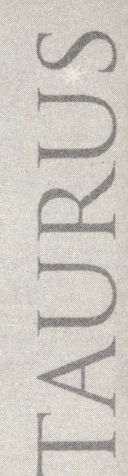

TAURUS

2009: Astronumerology

TAURUS

You give 100 percent in the first half of the game, and if that isn't enough in the second half you give what's left.

—Yogi Berra

The power behind your name

By adding the numbers of your name you can see which planet is ruling you. Each of the letters of the alphabet is assigned a number, which is tabled below. These numbers are ruled by the planets. This is according to the ancient Chaldean system of numerology and is very different to the Pythagorean system to which many refer.

Each number is assigned a planet:

AIQJY	=	1	**Sun**
BKR	=	2	**Moon**
CGLS	=	3	**Jupiter**
DMT	=	4	**Uranus**
EHNX	=	5	**Mercury**
UVW	=	6	**Venus**
OZ	=	7	**Neptune**
FP	=	8	**Saturn**
—	=	9	**Mars**

Notice that the number 9 is not allotted a letter because it is considered special. Once the numbers have been added you will see that a single planet rules your name and personal affairs. Many famous actors, writers and musicians change their names to attract the energy of a luckier planet. You can experiment with the table and try new names or add letters of your second name to see how that vibration suits you. It's a lot of fun!

2009: ASTRONUMEROLOGY

Here is an example of how to find out the power of your name. If your name is John Smith, calculate the ruling planet by correlating each letter to a number in the table like this:

J O H N   S M I T H

1 7 5 5   3 4 1 4 5

Now add the numbers like this:

1 + 7 + 5 + 5 + 3 + 4 + 1 + 4 + 5 = 35

Then add 3 + 5 = 8

The ruling number of John Smith's name is 8, which is ruled by Saturn. Now study the name-number table to reveal the power of your name. The numbers 3 and 5 will also play a secondary role in John's character and destiny so in this case you would also study the effects of Jupiter and Mercury.

Name-number table

Your name number	Ruling planet	Your name characteristics
1	Sun	Charismatic personality. Great vitality and life force. Physically active and outgoing. Attracts good friends and individuals in powerful positions. Good government connections. Intelligent, dramatic, showy and successful. A loyal number for relationships.
2	Moon	Soft, emotional temperament. Changeable moods but psychic, intuitive senses. Imaginative nature and compassionate expression of feelings. Loves family, mother and home life. Night owl who probably needs more sleep.

TAURUS

		Success with the public and/or the opposite sex.
3	Jupiter	Outgoing, optimistic number with lucky overtones. Attracts opportunities without trying. Good sense of timing. Religious or spiritual aspirations. Can investigate the meaning of life. Loves to travel and explore the world and people.
4	Uranus	Explosive personality with many quirky aspects. Likes the untried and untested. Forward thinking, with many unusual friends. Gets bored easily so needs plenty of stimulating experiences. Innovative, technological and creative. Wilful and stubborn when wants to be. Unexpected events in life may be positive or negative.
5	Mercury	Quick-thinking mind with great powers of speech. Extremely active life; always on the go and lives on nervous energy. Youthful attitude and never grows old. Looks younger than actual age. Young friends and humorous disposition. Loves reading and writing.
6	Venus	Charming personality. Graceful and attractive character, who cherishes friends and social life. Musical or artistic interests. Good for money making as well as numerous love affairs. Career in

2009: ASTRONUMEROLOGY

the public eye is possible. Loves family but is often overly concerned by friends.

7	Neptune	Intuitive, spiritual and self-sacrificing nature. Easily duped by those who need help. Loves to dream of life's possibilities. Has healing powers. Dreams are revealing and prophetic. Loves the water and will have many journeys in life. Spiritual aspirations dominate worldly desires.
8	Saturn	Hard-working, focused individual with slow but certain success. Incredible concentration and self-sacrifice for a goal. Money orientated but generous when trust is gained. Professional but may be a hard taskmaster. Demands highest standards and needs to learn to enjoy life a little more.
9	Mars	Incredible physical drive and ambition. Sports and outdoor activities are keys to health. Combative and likes to work and play just as hard. Protective of family, friends and territory. Individual tastes in life but is also self-absorbed. Needs to listen to others' advice to gain greater success.

TAURUS

Your 2009 planetary ruler

Astrology and numerology are closely linked. Each planet rules over a number between 1 and 9. Both your name and your birth date are ruled by planetary energies. Here are the planets and their ruling numbers:

1 Sun; 2 Moon; 3 Jupiter; 4 Uranus; 5 Mercury; 6 Venus; 7 Neptune; 8 Saturn; 9 Mars

Simply add the numbers of your birth date and the year in question to find out which planet will control the coming year for you. Here is an example:

If you were born on 12 November, add the numerals 1 and 2 (12, your day of birth) and 1 and 1 (11, your month of birth) to the year in question, in this case 2009 (current year), like this:

Add $1 + 2 + 1 + 1 + 2 + 0 + 0 + 9 = 16$

Then add these numbers again: $1 + 6 = 7$

The planet ruling your individual karma for 2009 will be Neptune because this planet rules the number 7.

You can even take your ruling name number as shown on page 113 and add it to the year in question to throw more light on your coming personal affairs like this:

John Smith = 8

Year coming = 2009

Add $8 + 2 + 0 + 0 + 9 = 19$

Add $1 + 9 = 10$

Add $1 + 0 = 1$

This is the ruling year number using your name number as a basis. Therefore, study the Sun's (number 1) influence for 2009. Enjoy!

2009: ASTRONUMEROLOGY

1 = Year of the Sun

Overview

The Sun is the brightest object in the heavens and rules number 1 and the sign of Leo. Because of this the coming year will bring you great success and popularity.

You'll be full of life and radiant vibrations and are more than ready to tackle your new nine-year cycle, which begins now. Any new projects you commence are likely to be successful.

Your health and vitality will be very strong and your stamina at its peak. Even if you happen to have the odd problem with your health, your recuperative power will be strong.

You have tremendous magnetism this year so social popularity won't be a problem for you. I see many new friends and lovers coming into your life. Expect loads of invitations to parties and fun-filled outings. Just don't take your health for granted as you're likely to burn the candle at both ends.

With success coming your way, don't let it go to your head. You must maintain humility, which will make you even more popular in the coming year.

Love and pleasure

This is an important cycle for renewing your love and connections with your family, particularly if you have children. The Sun is connected with the sign of Leo and therefore brings an increase in musical and theatrical activities. Entertainment and other creative hobbies will be high on your agenda and bring you a great sense of satisfaction.

Work

You won't have to make too much effort to be successful this year as the brightness of the Sun will draw opportunities to you. Changes in work are likely and if you have been concerned

TAURUS

that opportunities are few and far between, 2009 will be different. You can expect some sort of promotion or an increase in income because your employers will take special note of your skills and service orientation.

Improving your luck

Leo is the ruler of number 1 and therefore, if you're born under this star sign, 2009 will be particularly lucky. For others, July and August, the months of Leo, will bring good fortune. The 1st, 8th, 15th and 22nd hours of Sundays especially will give you a unique sort of luck in any sort of competition or activities generally. Keep your eye out for those born under Leo as they may be able to contribute something to your life and may even have a karmic connection to you. This is a particularly important year for your destiny.

Your lucky numbers in this coming cycle are 1, 10, 19 and 28.

2 = Year of the Moon

Overview

There's nothing more soothing than the cool light of the full Moon on a clear night. The Moon is emotional and receptive and controls your destiny in 2009. If you're able to use the positive energies of the Moon, it will be a great year in which you can realign and improve your relationships, particularly with family members.

Making a commitment to becoming a better person and bringing your emotions under control will also dominate your thinking. Try not to let your emotions get the better of you throughout the coming year because you may be drawn into the changeable nature of these lunar vibrations as well. If you fail to keep control of your emotional life you'll later regret some of your actions. You must carefully blend thinking with feeling to arrive at the best results. Your luck throughout 2009 will certainly be determined by the state of your mind.

2009: ASTRONUMEROLOGY

Because the Moon and the sign of Cancer rule the number 2 there is a certain amount of change to be expected this year. Keep your feelings steady and don't let your heart rule your head.

Love and pleasure

Your primary concern in 2009 will be your home and family life. You'll be keen to finally take on those renovations, or work on your garden. You may even think of buying a new home. You can at last carry out some of those plans and make your dreams come true. If you find yourself a little more temperamental than usual, do some extra meditation and spend time alone until you sort this out. You mustn't withhold your feelings from your partner as this will only create frustration.

Work

During 2009 your focus will be primarily on feelings and family; however, this doesn't mean you can't make great strides in your work as well. The Moon rules the general public and what you might find is that special opportunities and connections with the world at large present themselves to you. You could be working with large numbers of people.

If you're looking for a better work opportunity, try to focus your attention on women who can give you a hand. Use your intuition as it will be finely tuned this year. Work and career success depends upon your instincts.

Improving your luck

The sign of Cancer is your ruler this year and because the Moon rules Mondays, both this day of the week and the month of July are extremely lucky for you. The 1st, 8th, 15th and 22nd hours on Mondays will be very powerful. Pay special attention to the new and full Moon days throughout 2009.

The numbers 2, 11 and 29 are lucky for you.

TAURUS

3 = Year of Jupiter

Overview

The year 2009 will be a 3 year for you and, because of this, Jupiter and Sagittarius will dominate your affairs. This is very lucky and shows that you'll be motivated to broaden your horizons, gain more money and become extremely popular in your social circles. It looks like 2009 will be a fun-filled year with much excitement.

Jupiter and Sagittarius are generous to a fault and so likewise, your open-handedness will mark the year. You'll be friendly and helpful to all of those around you.

Pisces is also under the rulership of the number 3 and this brings out your spiritual and compassionate nature. You'll become a much better person, reducing your negative karma by increasing your self-awareness and spiritual feelings. You will want to share your luck with those you love.

Love and pleasure

Travel and seeking new adventures will be part and parcel of your romantic life this year. Travelling to distant lands and meeting unusual people will open your heart to fresh possibilities of romance.

You'll try novel and audacious things and will find yourself in a different circle of friends. Compromise will be important in making your existing relationships work. Talk about your feelings. If you are currently in a relationship you'll feel an upswing in your affection for your partner. This is a perfect opportunity to deepen your love for each other and take your relationship to a new level.

If you're not attached to someone just yet, there's good news for you. Great opportunities lie in store for you and a spiritual or karmic connection may be experienced in 2009.

Work

Great fortune can be expected through your working life in the next twelve months. Your friends and work colleagues will want to help you achieve your goals. Even your employers will be amenable to your requests for extra money or a better position within the organisation.

If you want to start a new job or possibly begin an independent line of business this is a great year to do it. Jupiter looks set to give you plenty of opportunities, success and a superior reputation.

Improving your luck

As long as you can keep a balanced view of things and not overdo anything, your luck will increase dramatically throughout 2009. The important thing is to remain grounded and not be too airy-fairy about your objectives. Be realistic about your talents and capabilities and don't brag about your skills or achievements. This will only invite envy from others.

Moderate your social life as well and don't drink or eat too much as this will slow your reflexes and lessen your chances for success.

You have plenty of spiritual insights this year so you should use them to their maximum. In the 1st, 8th, 15th and 24th hours of Thursdays you should use your intuition to enhance your luck, and the numbers 3, 12, 21 and 30 are also lucky for you. March and December are your lucky months but generally the whole year should go pretty smoothly for you.

4 = Year of Uranus

Overview

The electric and exciting planet of the zodiac Uranus and its sign of Aquarius rule your affairs throughout 2009. Dramatic

TAURUS

events will surprise and at the same time unnerve you in your professional and personal life. So be prepared!

You'll be able to achieve many things this year and your dreams are likely to come true, but you mustn't be distracted or scattered with your energies. You'll be breaking through your own self-limitations and this will present challenges from your family and friends. You'll want to be independent and develop your spiritual powers and nothing will stop you.

Try to maintain discipline and an orderly lifestyle so you can make the most of these special energies this year. If unexpected things do happen, it's not a bad idea to have an alternative plan so you don't lose momentum.

Love and pleasure

You want something radical, something different in your relationships this year. It's quite likely that your love life will be feeling a little less than exciting so you'll take some important steps to change that. If your partner is as progressive as you'll be this year, then your relationship is likely to improve and fulfil both of you.

In your social life you will meet some very unusual people whom you'll feel are specially connected to you spiritually. You may want to ditch everything for the excitement and passion of a completely new relationship, but tread carefully as this may not work out exactly as you'd expected.

Work

Technology, computing and the Internet will play a larger role in your professional life this coming year. You'll have to move ahead with the times and learn new skills if you want to achieve success.

A hectic schedule is likely, so make sure your diary is with you at all times. Try to be more efficient and don't waste time.

2009: ASTRONUMEROLOGY

New friends and alliances at work will help you achieve even greater success in the coming period. Becoming a team player will be even more important towards gaining satisfaction in your professional endeavours.

Improving your luck

Moving too quickly and impulsively will cause you problems on all fronts, so be a little more patient and think your decisions through more carefully. Social, romantic and professional opportunities will come to you but take a little time to investigate the ramifications of your actions.

The 1st, 8th, 15th and 20th hours of any Saturday are lucky, but love and luck are likely to cross your path when you least expect it. The numbers 4, 13, 22 and 31 are also lucky for you this year.

5 = Year of Mercury

Overview

The supreme planet of communication, Mercury, is your ruling planet throughout 2009. The number 5, which is connected to Mercury, will confer upon you success through your intellectual abilities.

Any form of writing or speaking will be improved and this will be, to a large extent, underpinning your success. Your imagination will be stimulated by this planet with many incredible new and exciting ideas coming to mind.

Mercury and the number 5 are considered somewhat indecisive. Be firm in your attitude and don't let too many ideas or opportunities distract and confuse you. By all means get as much information as you can to help you make the right decision.

I see you involved with money proposals, job applications, even contracts that need to be signed so remain clear-headed as much as possible.

TAURUS

Your business skills and clear and concise communication will be at the heart of your life in 2009.

Love and pleasure

Mercury, which rules the signs of Gemini and Virgo, will make your love life a little difficult due to its changeable nature. On the one hand you'll feel passionate and loving to your partner, yet on the other you will feel like giving it all up for the excitement of a new affair. Maintain the middle ground.

Also, try not to be too critical with your friends and family members. The influence of Virgo makes you prone to expecting much more from others than they're capable of giving. Control your sharp tongue and don't hurt people's feelings. Encouraging others is the better path, leading to more emotional satisfaction.

Work

Speed will dominate your professional life in 2009. You'll be flitting from one subject to another and taking on far more than you can handle. You'll need to make some serious changes in your routine to handle the avalanche of work that will come your way. You'll also be travelling with your work, but not necessarily overseas.

If you're in a job you enjoy then this year will give you additional successes. If not, it may be time to move on.

Improving your luck

Communication is the secret of attaining your desires in the coming twelve months. Keep focused on one idea rather than scattering your energies in all directions and your success will be speedier.

By looking after your health, sleeping well and exercising regularly, you'll build up your resilience and mental strength.

The 1st, 8th, 15th and 20th hours of Wednesday are lucky so it's best to schedule your meetings and other important social engagements during these times. The lucky numbers for Mercury are 5, 14, 23 and 32.

6 = Year of Venus

Overview

Because you're ruled by 6 this year, love is in the air! Venus, Taurus and Libra are well known for their affinity with romance, love, and even marriage. If ever you were going to meet a soulmate and feel comfortable in love, 2009 must surely be your year.

Taurus has a strong connection to money and practical affairs as well, so finances will also improve if you are diligent about work and security issues.

The important thing to keep in mind this year is that sharing love and making that important soul connection should be kept high on your agenda. This will be an enjoyable period in your life.

Love and pleasure

Romance is the key thing for you this year and your current relationships will become more fulfilling if you happen to be attached. For singles, a 6 year heralds an important meeting that eventually leads to marriage.

You'll also be interested in fashion, gifts, jewellery and all sorts of socialising. It's at one of these social engagements that you could meet the love of your life. Remain available!

Venus is one of the planets that has a tendency to overdo things, so be moderate in your eating and drinking. Try generally to maintain a modest lifestyle.

TAURUS

Work

You'll have a clearer insight into finances and your future security during a number 6 year. Whereas you may have had additional expenses and extra distractions previously, your mind will be more settled and capable of longer-term planning along these lines.

With the extra cash you might see this year, decorating your home or office will give you a special sort of satisfaction.

Social affairs and professional activities will be strongly linked. Any sort of work-related functions may offer you romantic opportunities as well. On the other hand, be careful not to mix up your workplace relationships with romantic ideals. This could complicate some of your professional activities.

Improving your luck

You'll want more money and a life of leisure and ease in 2009. Keep working on your strengths and eliminate your negative personality traits to create greater luck and harmony in your life.

Moderate all your actions and don't focus exclusively on money and material objects. Feed your spiritual needs as well. By balancing the inner and outer you'll see that your romantic and professional life will be enhanced more easily.

The 1st, 8th, 15th and 20th hours on Fridays will be very lucky for you and new opportunities will arise for you at those times. You can use the numbers 6, 15, 24 and 33 to increase luck in your general affairs.

7 = Year of Neptune

Overview

The last and most evolved sign of the zodiac is Pisces, which is ruled by Neptune. The number 7 is deeply connected with this

2009: ASTRONUMEROLOGY

zodiacal sign and governs you in 2009. Your ideals seem to be clearer and more spiritually orientated than ever before. Your desire to evolve and understand your inner self will be a double-edged sword. It depends on how organised you are as to how well you can use these spiritual and abstract concepts in your practical life.

Your past emotional hurts and deep emotional issues will be dealt with and removed for good, if you are serious about becoming a better human being.

Spend a little more time caring for yourself rather than others, as it's likely some of your friends will drain you of energy with their own personal problems. Of course, you mustn't turn a blind eye to the needs of others, but don't ignore your own personal needs in the process.

Love and pleasure

Meeting people with similar life views and spiritual aspirations will rekindle your faith in relationships. If you do choose to develop a new romance, make sure that there is a clear understanding of the responsibilities of one to the other. Don't get swept off your feet by people who have ulterior motives.

Keep your relationships realistic and see that the most idealistic partnerships must eventually come down to Earth. Deal with the practicalities of life.

Work

This is a year of hard work, but one in which you'll come to understand the deeper significance of your professional ideals. You may discover a whole new aspect to your career, which involves a more compassionate and self-sacrificing side to your personality.

You'll also find that your way of working will change and that you'll be more focused and able to get into the spirit of

TAURUS

whatever you do. Finding meaningful work is very likely and therefore this could be a year when money, security, creativity and spirituality overlap to bring you a great sense of personal satisfaction.

Tapping into your greater self through meditation and self-study will bring you great benefits throughout 2009.

Improving your luck

Using self-sacrifice along with discrimination will be an unusual method of improving your luck. The laws of karma state that what you give, you receive in greater measure. This is one of the principal themes for you in 2009.

The 1st, 8th, 15th and 20th hours of Tuesdays are your lucky times. The numbers 7, 16, 25 and 34 should be used to increase your lucky energies.

8 = Year of Saturn

Overview

The earthy and practical sign of Capricorn and its ruler Saturn are intimately linked to the number 8, which rules you in 2009. Your discipline and far-sightedness will help you achieve great things in the coming year. With cautious discernment, slowly but surely you will reach your goals.

It may be that due to the influence of the solitary Saturn, your best work and achievement will be behind closed doors away from the limelight. You mustn't fear this as you'll discover many new things about yourself. You'll learn just how strong you really are.

Love and pleasure

Work will overshadow your personal affairs in 2009, but you mustn't let this erode the personal relationships you have. Becoming a workaholic brings great material successes but will also cause you to become too insular and aloof. Your family members won't take too kindly to you working 100-hour weeks.

Responsibility is one of the key words for this number and you will therefore find yourself in a position of authority that leaves very little time for fun. Try to make time to enjoy the company of friends and family and by all means schedule time off on the weekends as it will give you the peace of mind you're looking for.

Because of your responsible attitude it will be very hard for you not to assume a greater role in your workplace and this indicates longer working hours with the likelihood of a promotion with equally good remuneration.

Work

Money is high on your agenda in 2009. Number 8 is a good money number according to the Chinese and this year is at last likely to bring you the fruits of your hard labour. You are cautious and resourceful in all your dealings and will not waste your hard-earned savings. You will also be very conscious of using your time wisely.

You will be given more responsibilities and you're likely to take them on, if only to prove to yourself that you can handle whatever life dishes up.

Expect a promotion in which you will play a leading role in your work. Your diligence and hard work will pay off, literally, in a bigger salary and more respect from others.

Improving your luck

Caution is one of the key characteristics of the number 8 and is linked to Capricorn. But being overly cautious could cause you to miss valuable opportunities. If an offer is put to you, try to think outside the square and balance it with your naturally cautious nature.

TAURUS

Be gentle and kind to yourself. By loving yourself, others will naturally love you, too. The 1st, 8th, 15th and 20th hours of Saturdays are exceptionally lucky for you as are the numbers 1, 8, 17, 26 and 35.

9 = Year of Mars

Overview

You are now entering the final year of a nine-year cycle dominated by the planet Mars and the sign of Aries. You'll be completing many things and are determined to be successful after several years of intense work.

Some of your relationships may now have reached their use-by date and even these personal affairs may need to be released. Don't let arguments and disagreements get in the road of friendly resolution in these areas of your life.

Mars is a challenging planet and, this year, although you will be very active and productive, you may find others trying to obstruct the achievement of your goals. As a result you may react strongly to them, thereby creating disharmony in your workplace. Don't be so impulsive or reckless, and generally slow things down. The slower, steadier approach has greater merit this year.

Love and pleasure

If you become too bossy and pushy with friends this year you will just end up pushing them out of your life. It's a year to end certain friendships but by the same token it could be the perfect time to end conflicts and thereby bolster your love affairs in 2009.

If you're feeling a little irritable and angry with those you love, try getting rid of these negative feelings through some intense, rigorous sports and physical activity. This will definitely relieve tension and improve your personal life.

Work

Because you're healthy and able to work at a more intense pace you'll achieve an incredible amount in the coming year. Overwork could become a problem if you're not careful.

Because the number 9 and Mars are infused with leadership energy, you'll be asked to take the reins of the job and steer your company or group in a certain direction. This will bring with it added responsibility but also a greater sense of purpose for you.

Improving your luck

Because of the hot and restless energy of the number 9, it is important to create more mental peace in your life this year. Lower the temperature, so to speak, and decompress your relationships rather than becoming aggravated. Try to talk to your work partners and loved ones rather than telling them what to do. This will generally pick up your health and your relationships

The 1st, 8th, 15th and 20th hours of Tuesdays are the luckiest for you this year and, if you're involved in any disputes or need to attend to health issues, these times are also very good for the best results. Your lucky numbers are 9, 18, 27 and 36

# TAURUS

2009:
Your Daily Planner

> *Great works are performed, not by strength, but by perseverance.*
>
> —Samuel Johnson

There is a little-known branch of astrology called electional astrology, and it can help you select the most appropriate times for many of your day-to-day activities.

Ancient astrologers understood the planetary patterns and how they impacted on each of us. This allowed them to suggest the best possible times to start various important activities. Many farmers today still use this approach: they understand the phases of the Moon, and attest to the fact that planting seeds on certain lunar days produces a far better crop than planting on other days.

The following section covers many areas of daily life, and uses the cycles of the Moon and the combined strength of the other planets to work out the best times to start different types of activity.

So to create your own personal almanac, first select the activity you are interested in, and then quickly scan the year for the best months to start it. When you have selected the month, you can finetune your timing by finding the best specific dates. You can then be sure that the planetary energies will be in sync with you, offering you the best possible outcome.

Coupled with what you know about your monthly and weekly trends, the daily planner can be a powerful tool to help you capitalise on opportunities that come your way this year.

Good luck, and may the planets bless you with great success, fortune and happiness in 2009!

Starting activities

How many times have you made a new year's resolution to begin a diet or be a better person in your relationships? And how many times has it not worked out? Well, the reason may be partly that you started out at the wrong time! How successful you are is strongly influenced by the position of the Moon and the planets when you begin a particular activity. You could be more successful with the following activities if you start them on the days indicated.

Relationships

We all feel more empowered on some days than on others. This is because the planets have some power over us—their movement and their relationships to each other determine the ebb and flow of our energies. And our level of self-confidence and our sense of romantic magnetism play an important part in the way we behave in relationships.

Your daily planner tells you the ideal dates for meeting new friends, initiating a love affair, spending time with family and loved ones—it even tells you the most appropriate times for sexual encounters.

You'll be surprised at how much more impact you make in your relationships when you tune yourself in to the planetary energies on these special dates.

Falling in love/restoring love

During these times you could expect favourable energies to meet your soulmate or, if you've had difficulty in a relationship, to approach the one you love to rekindle both your and their emotional responses:

January	28, 30
February	25, 26
March	6, 7, 8, 28, 29, 30
April	25, 26, 30
May	1, 2, 5, 7, 26, 27, 28, 29

TAURUS

June	2, 3, 23, 24, 26, 29, 30
July	22, 23, 26, 27
August	14, 15, 16, 17, 22, 23, 24
September	10, 14, 16, 19, 20, 21
October	9, 10, 11, 12, 13
November	25, 26
December	22, 23, 27, 31

Special times with friends and family

Socialising, partying and having a good time with those you enjoy being with is highly favourable under the following dates. These dates are excellent to spend time with family and loved ones in a domestic environment:

January	26
February	8, 12, 13, 14, 22, 23, 24
March	8, 22, 23
April	19, 27, 28
May	1, 2, 15, 16, 17, 24, 25, 28, 29
June	2, 3, 11, 12, 13, 22, 30
July	23, 26, 27
August	5, 6, 23, 24
September	16
October	13
November	8, 10, 24
December	19, 20, 21, 29

2009: YOUR DAILY PLANNER

Healing or resuming relationships

If you're trying to get back together with the one you love and need a heart-to-heart or deep and meaningful, you can try the following dates to do so:

January	5, 8, 11, 12, 18, 19, 20, 21, 22, 23, 24, 25, 26, 28, 30
February	8, 12, 13, 14
March	8
April	18, 19
May	1, 2, 28, 29
June	2, 3, 30
July	23, 26, 27
August	23, 24
September	16
October	13
November	8
December	22, 23, 27

Sexual encounters

Physical and sexual energies are well favoured on the following dates. The energies of the planets enhance your moments of intimacy during these times:

January	5, 30
February	25, 26
March	6, 7, 8, 28, 29, 30
April	25, 26, 30
May	1, 2, 5, 7, 26, 27, 28, 29

TAURUS

June	2, 3, 23, 24, 26, 29, 30
July	22, 23, 26, 27
August	23, 24
September	16
October	13
November	25, 26
December	22, 23, 27, 31

Health and wellbeing

Your aura and life force are susceptible to the movements of the planets; in particular, they respond to the phases of the Moon.

The following dates are the most appropriate times to begin a diet, have cosmetic surgery, or seek medical advice. They also tell you when the best times are to help others.

Feeling of wellbeing

Your physical as well as your mental alertness should be strong on these following dates. You can plan your activities and expect a good response from others:

January	8, 9, 26, 27
February	4, 5, 22, 23
March	31
April	18, 19, 27, 28
May	16, 17
June	21, 22
July	19
August	5, 6, 24, 25

September	12, 28, 30
October	8, 9
November	8, 10
December	19, 20, 21, 29, 30

Healing and medicine

This is good for approaching others who have expertise at a time when you need some deeper understanding. This is also favourable for any sort of healing or medication and making appointments with doctors or psychologists. Planning surgery around these dates should bring good results.

Often giving up our time and energy to assist others doesn't necessarily result in the expected outcome. By lending a helping hand to a friend on the following dates, the results should be favourable:

January	1, 20, 21, 22, 23, 24, 25, 26, 27, 28, 29, 30, 31
February	9, 10, 11, 12, 13, 14, 15, 16, 17, 18, 19, 20, 21, 22, 23, 24, 25, 26, 27, 28
March	2, 3, 4, 5, 6, 7, 8, 9, 22, 26, 28, 29, 30, 31
April	1, 10, 12, 15, 18, 20, 27, 28, 29, 30
May	1, 3, 7, 8, 9, 10, 11, 12
June	6, 7, 9, 13, 14, 15, 19, 21, 22
July	5, 6, 7, 8, 10, 12, 18, 19, 20, 25, 26
August	6, 7, 8, 9, 10, 29, 30, 31
September	1, 6, 27
October	8, 9, 10, 11, 12, 25, 26
November	18, 19, 20, 21, 22
December	10, 11, 12

TAURUS

Money

Money is an important part of life, and involves many decisions; decisions about borrowing, investing, spending. The ideal times for transactions are very much influenced by the planets, and whether your investment or nest egg grows or doesn't grow can often be linked to timing. Making your decisions on the following dates could give you a whole new perspective on your financial future.

Managing wealth and money

To build your nest egg, it's a good time to open your bank account and invest money on the following dates:

January	3, 4, 5, 10, 11, 16, 17, 23, 24, 25, 31
February	1, 6, 7, 12, 13, 14, 20, 21, 27, 28
March	5, 6, 7, 12, 13, 19, 26, 27
April	2, 3, 8, 9, 15, 17, 23, 24, 29, 30
May	5, 6, 7, 13, 14, 20, 21, 26, 27
June	2, 3, 9, 10, 16, 17, 18, 23, 24, 29, 30
July	6, 7, 8, 14, 15, 20, 21, 26, 27
August	2, 3, 4, 10, 11, 17, 18, 23, 24, 30, 31
September	6, 7, 13, 14, 19, 20, 26, 27
October	3, 4, 5, 10, 11, 16, 17, 18, 23, 24, 25, 31
November	1, 6, 7, 13, 14, 20, 21, 27, 28
December	4, 5, 10, 11, 17, 18, 24, 25, 26, 31

Spending

It's always fun to spend but the following dates are more in tune with this activity and are likely to give you better results:

January	20, 28, 30
February	3
March	28, 29, 30
April	25, 26
May	31
June	1, 2, 7, 8, 9, 10, 28, 30
July	1, 2, 3, 26, 27, 29, 30
August	2, 3, 4, 5, 20, 21, 22, 23, 24, 25
September	19, 20, 21, 22, 23
October	9, 10
November	1, 7, 8, 17
December	27, 28

Selling

If you're thinking of selling something, whether it is small or large, consider the following dates as ideal times to do so:

January	3, 18, 19, 20, 21, 25, 26, 27, 28, 29, 30, 31
February	8, 10, 11, 12, 13, 14, 15, 18, 20, 22, 23, 24, 26, 28
March	2, 3, 4, 5, 6, 7, 8, 9, 16, 26, 27, 28, 31
April	5, 10, 19, 20, 23, 25, 27, 28, 29
May	1, 2, 7, 9, 13, 14, 21, 24, 25, 28, 29, 31
June	1, 2, 7, 8, 14, 16, 17, 20, 21, 22, 26, 30
July	1, 2, 3, 9, 10, 11, 15, 16, 17, 26, 27
August	2, 3, 4, 13, 14, 15, 16, 17
September	1, 2, 3, 4, 5, 6, 14, 15, 16, 17, 21, 22, 23, 24, 25, 26, 27, 28, 30, 31

TAURUS

October	1, 2, 3, 4, 5, 6, 7, 8, 9, 10, 11, 12, 31
November	2, 3, 9, 10, 11, 12, 13, 25, 26, 27, 28, 29, 30
December	1, 2, 3, 7, 8, 9, 17, 20

Borrowing

Few of us like to borrow money, but if you must, taking out a loan on the following dates should be positive:

January	11, 18, 19, 20, 23, 24, 25
February	15, 16, 20, 21
March	14, 15, 19, 20
April	10, 11, 12, 15, 16, 17
May	9, 13, 14
June	9, 10
July	7, 8, 20, 21
August	17, 18
September	13, 14
October	10, 11
November	6, 7, 15, 16
December	4, 5, 12, 13, 14

Work and education

Your career is important to you, and continual improvement of your skills is therefore also crucial, professionally, mentally and socially. The dates below will help you find out the most appropriate times to improve your professional talents and commence new work or education associated with your work.

You may need to decide when to start learning a new skill, when to ask for a promotion, and even when to make an

2009: YOUR DAILY PLANNER

important career change. Here are the days when mental and educational power is strong.

Learning new skills

Educational pursuits are lucky and bring good results on the following dates:

January	8, 9
February	4, 5
March	3, 4, 10, 31
April	1, 6, 7, 27, 28
May	3, 4, 25, 30, 31
June	1, 6, 7, 27, 28
July	4, 5, 24, 25, 31
August	1, 21, 22, 27, 28, 29
September	23, 24, 25
October	21, 22
November	17, 18, 19
December	29, 30

Changing career path or profession

If you're feeling stuck and need to move into a new professional activity, changing jobs can be done at these times:

January	6, 7
February	2, 3
March	1, 2, 3, 4, 5, 6, 7, 8, 9, 10, 28, 29, 30
April	6, 7, 25, 26
May	3, 4, 30, 31
June	1, 27, 28

TAURUS

July	6, 24, 25
August	2, 3, 4, 21, 22, 30, 31
September	26, 27
October	23, 24, 25
November	2, 20, 21, 29, 30
December	1, 17, 18, 27, 28

Promotion, professional focus and hard work

To increase your mental focus and achieve good results from the work you do, promotions are likely on these dates that follow:

January	4, 5, 6, 11, 12, 13, 14, 15, 16, 21
February	6
March	18, 19, 20
April	8, 28, 29
May	12, 21
June	25, 26
July	1, 2, 3, 8, 15, 17
August	4, 14, 15, 16, 17, 18, 22, 23, 24
September	14, 15, 18, 19, 23, 24, 25, 26
October	22
November	7, 10, 11, 12, 17
December	1, 2, 3, 7, 28

Travel

Setting out on a holiday or adventurous journey is exciting. To gain the most out of your holidays and journeys, travelling on the following dates is likely to give you a sense of fulfilment:

January	9, 10, 28, 29, 30, 31
February	1, 4, 5, 26
March	3, 4, 5, 6, 7, 27, 31
April	27, 28, 29
May	1, 2, 25
June	6, 7, 25, 26
July	6, 31
August	1, 2, 21, 22, 23, 24, 29
September	19, 20, 23, 24, 25, 26, 27
October	1, 2, 3, 25, 28, 29, 30, 31
November	1, 17, 18, 26, 28
December	17, 18, 23, 26

Beauty and grooming

Believe it or not, cutting your hair or nails has a powerful effect on your body's electromagnetic energy. If you cut your hair or nails at the wrong time of the month, you can reduce your level of vitality significantly. Use these dates to ensure you optimise your energy levels by staying in tune with the stars.

Hair and nails

January	1, 2, 8, 9, 21, 22, 28, 29, 30
February	4, 5, 17, 18, 19, 25, 26
March	3, 4, 16, 17, 18, 24, 25, 31
April	1, 13, 14, 20, 21, 22, 27, 28, 29, 30
May	8, 10, 11, 12, 18, 19, 24, 25
June	6, 7, 8, 14, 15, 21, 22

TAURUS

July	4, 5, 11, 12, 13, 18, 19, 31
August	1, 7, 8, 9, 14, 15, 16, 27, 28, 29
September	4, 5, 11, 12, 23, 24, 25
October	1, 2, 8, 9, 21, 22, 28, 29, 30
November	4, 5, 17, 18, 19, 25, 26
December	2, 3, 15, 16, 22, 23, 29, 30

Therapies, massage and self-pampering

January	18, 19, 20, 26, 27
February	3, 6, 7, 8, 12, 13, 14, 15, 16, 22, 23, 24
March	6, 8, 28, 29, 30
April	5, 8, 9, 18, 19, 25, 26, 29, 30
May	1, 2, 5, 7, 9, 15, 16, 17, 22, 23, 26, 27, 28, 29
June	2, 3, 4, 5, 11, 12, 13, 19, 20, 23, 24, 26, 30
July	1, 2, 3, 9, 10, 23, 26, 27, 28, 29, 30
August	6, 12, 13, 17, 18, 19, 20, 23, 24, 25, 26
September	1, 2, 13, 14, 16
October	10, 11, 12, 13, 16, 17, 27
November	8, 9, 10, 13, 16, 23, 24, 29, 30
December	1, 4, 5, 6, 7, 10, 11, 12, 13, 14, 19, 20, 21, 27, 28, 31

MILLS & BOON
MODERN

...International affairs, seduction and passion guaranteed

The Greek Tycoon's Pregnant Wife
Anne Mather

Miranda Lee
Blackmailed into the Italian's Bed

8 brand-new titles each month

Available on the first Friday of every month
from WHSmith, ASDA, Tesco
and all good bookshops
www.millsandboon.co.uk

GEN/01/RTL11

MILLS & BOON
MODERN
Heat

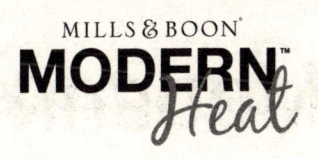

If you like Mills & Boon Modern you'll love Modern Heat!

Strong, sexy alpha heroes, sizzling storylines and exotic locations from around the world – what more could you want!

2 brand-new titles each month

Available on the first Friday of every month
from WHSmith, ASDA, Tesco
and all good bookshops
www.millsandboon.co.uk

MILLS & BOON
Romance

Pure romance, pure emotion

4 brand-new titles each month

Available on the first Friday of every month
from WHSmith, ASDA, Tesco
and all good bookshops
www.millsandboon.co.uk

MILLS & BOON
MEDICAL

**Pulse-raising romance –
Heart-racing medical drama**

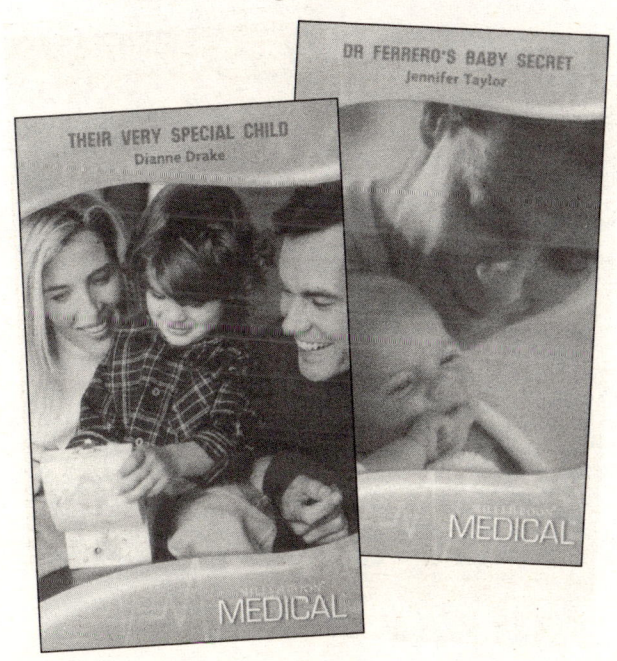

6 brand-new titles each month

Available on the first Friday of every month
from WHSmith, ASDA, Tesco
and all good bookshops
www.millsandboon.co.uk

GEN/03/RTL11

MILLS & BOON
Historical

Rich, vivid and passionate

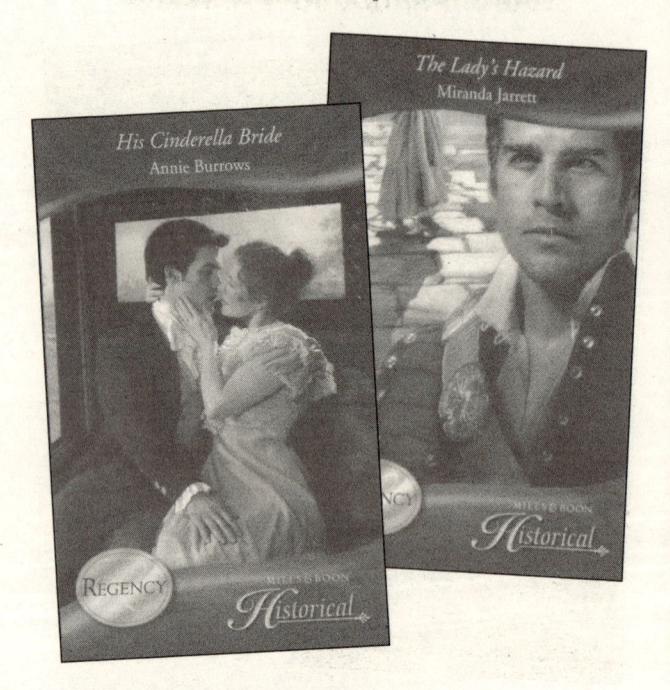

4 brand-new titles each month

Available on the first Friday of every month
from WHSmith, ASDA, Tesco
and all good bookshops
www.millsandboon.co.uk

GEN/04/RTL11

MILLS & BOON
Blaze

Scorching hot sexy reads...

GOING ALL THE WAY
Isobel Sharpe

HIDDEN OBSESSION
Joanne Rock

4 brand-new titles each month

Available on the first Friday of every month
from WHSmith, ASDA, Tesco
and all good bookshops
www.millsandboon.co.uk

GEN/14/RTL11

MILLS & BOON
Special Edition

Life, love and family

6 brand-new titles each month

Available on the third Friday of every month
from WHSmith, ASDA, Tesco
and all good bookshops
www.millsandboon.co.uk

MILLS & BOON
SuperROMANCE

Enjoy the drama, explore the emotions, experience the relationships

4 brand-new titles each month

Available on the third Friday of every month
from WHSmith, ASDA, Tesco
and all good bookshops
www.millsandboon.co.uk

GEN/38/RTL11

MILLS & BOON
INTRIGUE

Breathtaking romance & adventure

8 brand-new titles each month

Available on the third Friday of every month
from WHSmith, ASDA, Tesco
and all good bookshops
www.millsandboon.co.uk

GEN/46/RTL11

MILLS & BOON
Desire™ 2-in-1

2 passionate, dramatic love stories in each book

3 brand-new titles to choose from each month

Available on the third Friday of every month from WHSmith, ASDA, Tesco and all good bookshops
www.millsandboon.co.uk

Celebrate our centenary year with 24 special short stories!

ONLY £1.49! EACH

A special 100th Birthday Collection from your favourite authors including:

Penny Jordan • Diana Palmer • Lucy Gordon
Carole Mortimer • Betty Neels
Debbie Macomber • Sharon Kendrick
Alexandra Sellers • Nicola Cornick

Two stories published every month from January 2008 to January 2009

Collect all 24 stories to complete the set!

MILLS & BOON®
Pure reading pleasure

www.millsandboon.co.uk